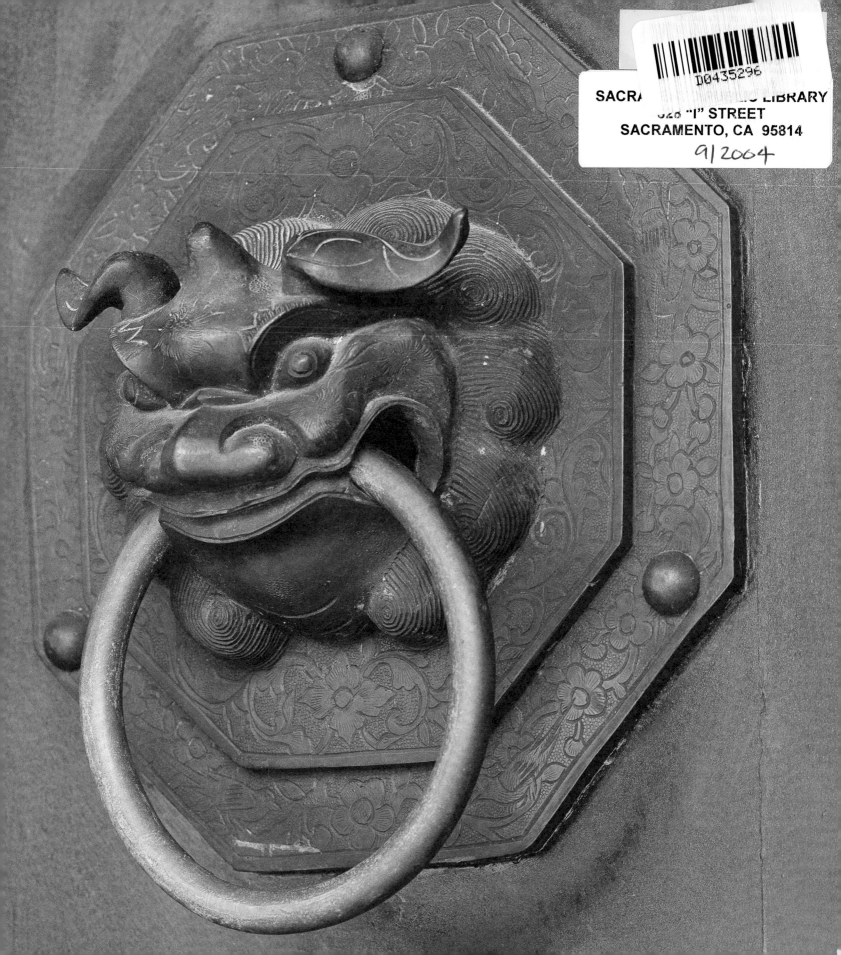

FENG SHUI STYLE

The Asian Art of Gracious Living

Stephen Skinner

photographs by Graham Price

PERIPLUS

Published by Periplus Editions
with editorial offices at
130 Joo Seng Rd, #06-01,
Singapore 368357

ISBN 0 7946 0231 2

Design: Mind Design
Printed in Singapore

Distributed by:
*North America, Latin America
and Europe*
Tuttle Publishing,
364 Innovation Drive,
North Clarendon, VT 05759-9436
Tel (802) 773 8930
Fax (802) 773 6993
Email: info@tuttlepublishing.com
www.tuttlepublishing.com

Asia Pacific
Berkeley Books Pte Ltd,
130 Joo Seng Road #06-01/03,
Singapore 368357
Tel (65) 6280 1330
Fax (65) 6280 6290
Email: inquiries@periplus.com.sg

Japan
Tuttle Publishing,
Yaekari Building, 3F, 5-4-12 Osaki,
Shinagawa-ku, Tokyo 141-0032
Tel (813) 5437 0171
Fax (813) 5437 0755
Email: tuttle-sales@gol.com

Front cover: A touch of beige in the
Beluga bedroom at The Hempel, with
sunlight and *yang* energy, streaming in
through the windows.

This page: Buddha heads are a recur-
ring theme at China White in London.
They provide not just a talking point
but also an anchor to the design of
the room. Buddhism has however, no
direct connection with feng shui. In
fact, many orthodox Buddhists frown
upon the practice. If feng shui has
any religious roots then they are in
the indigenous Taoist religion, rather
than Buddhism.

CONTENTS

THE ANCIENT ART OF HARMONIOUS LIVING

Feng shui is the ancient Chinese art of arranging the architecture, design and furnishings of a building to harmonize with its surroundings, in order to improve the success, health, wealth and happiness of the people living and working in that building. Designers and architects also have the same objectives—to create living spaces that are as congenial as possible for their clients. Good architecture and good interior design should invariably produce a living space in which the client feels comfortable and able to work efficiently, and of course, remains healthy.

Feng shui literally means "wind-water," and so many of its basic principles relate to these two elements. The direction of the prevailing breeze, and how best to trap this to cool or refresh the house, is a common concern of feng shui practitioners, designers and architects. Water is even more important, and the siting of any pool, from the smallest fountain to the largest swimming pool, is very important both for aesthetic and feng shui reasons. The swimming pool especially should not overwhelm the house, but fit into the surrounding landscape in a way that supports the house. Feng shui is also concerned with details like the direction the water enters the pool, and where its exit is located. This is because water carries with it *ch'i* energy.

For different reasons, but often with the same effect, architects will seek (in the Northern Hemisphere) to angle the house to the South or SE, catching the early morning warmth of the sun's rising. Traditional feng shui also sees these as good facing directions. Of course there are other concerns which govern house facing direction in feng shui, such as the birth date of the owner or the time period in which the house is to be built (discussed further in the "Principles of Feng Shui" section).

Both design and feng shui are concerned with the relationship between the building being designed and its surrounding countryside, landforms, and buildings. Feng shui suggests that it is harmful to the occupants of a house to have, for example two large nearby buildings looming over the house. From an architectural point of view, it is obvious that anything blocking out the sun is a significant downside to any site. Also, no architect wants his work diminished by comparison with its neighbor.

Another major part of feng shui that strives hard to eliminate shapes or forms which generate unsettling energies, is the art of alignment. From the feng shui perspective, any large sharp corner or ugly object facing the home under consideration, is damaging to the occupants of that home. Similarly, from a design point of view, nobody wants to overlook or be overlooked by an unattractive neighboring structure. Both designer and feng shui master would strive to screen off the offending object.

Good design, be it of a building or single room, is about creating something in an efficient and beautiful manner and designing it with a liberal dash of inventiveness or originality. Spaces that are visually delightful and promote harmony, health and a feeling of well-being are often the result of both good design and good feng shui.

Feng shui has long been concerned with all these objectives, plus a few more. The basis of all feng shui is the harmonious balancing of *yin* and *yang*. A feng shui master strives to generate and accumulate healthy energetic *ch'i*. Just as a good interior designer will balance light and dark shades, a feng shui master will look for a balance between bright open spaces (*yang*) and quiet dark spaces (*yin*). He will attempt to position quiet, less used rooms, like spare bedrooms or storerooms in areas of inauspicious *ch'i*, and will site main bedrooms, living and dining areas and workrooms in areas of *sheng ch'i* or vibrant strong energy. Likewise, an architect will place the main living areas towards the front of a house, and the service areas at the back. Obviously, not every architectural rule will find a corresponding rule under feng shui. For example it is considered a bad feng shui idea to site a kitchen in the NW corner of a house, a concept that would not necessarily deter an architect from doing the same.

The creation of a home that will promote energy and preserve health is another consideration of both good design and good feng shui. Feng shui has always had a healthy respect for good drainage. Just as water helps to carry *ch'i* energy, foul water carries *sha ch'i* energy. Drains and water exit points are often covered or disguised, which is a good general principle from a health point of view.

Ventilation is another health-related area where both would agree: the accumulation of condensation or stagnant air is a definite feng shui no-no. The circulation of air is

Right: The reception area is very *yin* although it appears to be *yang*, as it is cavernous and starkly pure white. Ideally, it should have a balance of *yin* and *yang*, with *yang* in the ascendancy as it is a public area.

especially important in the tropics where high moisture levels need adequate ventilation. Even more to the point, sweet air which is not too strong and gusty or too stagnant, is an essential requirement of feng shui. Tropical living has produced homes that are really just a collection of rooms built as a series of pavilions connected by covered walkways, allowing for the free flow of air. These will often have water built in as part of the design. In these cases, the feng shui of each pavilion must be judged separately.

Feng shui is rooted in our surrounding landscape. City living has however, narrowed our perceptions so much that we no longer see the effect that landscape and garden has on the feng shui of a building. In the city, the most natural landscape that can be hoped for is a garden. Thus, the importance of engineering the feng shui of any surrounding garden must also be considered.

Although not identical, good design and feng shui work hand in hand to produce living spaces that are both beautiful and beneficial to their owners. A well-designed space often incorporates many of the rules of placement that are an integral part of feng shui. A good designer will place furniture so that there is an easy path through and convenient access to each part of a room. A feng shui practitioner will ensure that there are no dark or cramped corners that could trap energy. To do this, he makes sure there are clear paths for the *ch'i* to flow, and after determining the flow and type of *ch'i* energy present in the building, modifies and improves it accordingly.

Where buildings have been constructed or furnished consciously with feng shui rules in mind, the resulting design often reflects this. On the other hand, there are many well-designed buildings that have unconsciously tapped into good feng shui (without specific input from a feng shui master) and this is reflected in the life and outlook of their occupants. In a way, every building has something to tell us about feng shui.

In putting this book together, I have had to think long and hard about the many ways that feng shui has affected the design of the places included in this book. The popular western concept of feng shui, inculcated by more than 20 years of western books on the subject, is one of minimalism, purity and emptiness, with an implied spirituality. However, far from being solely spiritual, feng shui is concerned with the improvement of life here and now, and its objectives include business success and the generation of wealth. In actual fact, feng shui as practiced in China and other areas of Asia is much more practical and does not always produce the clean lines associated with minimalism or Zen. They nonetheless produce richly productive rooms, where one feels totally at ease in.

Design concepts made by traditional Chinese feng shui practitioners are not concerned with minimalism, but with the facing direction of the building, the location of water in and near the building, the position of the main door and other entrances, the uses to which particular rooms are put, and the effect of these factors upon different members of the family (or team in the case of an office) living or working there. I have deliberately selected a wide range of examples of feng shui design—from that practiced by well respected masters from the late Ch'ing dynasty (as in the Cheong Fatt Tze mansion) to modern interpretations of feng shui found in high-tech buildings created in the late 20th century, like the Hempel. The principles however, are timeless.

In some cases, a feng shui practitioner or master will have analyzed the structure and offered his suggestions at the design and construction stage: this is common practice in Hong Kong today. Sometimes, feng shui changes will have been carried out only after construction. In other cases although the building has been designed by an architect without a formal knowledge of feng shui, he has fitted the building into the landscape in such a way as to take advantage, albeit unwittingly, of excellent feng shui benefits.

Accordingly, in this book you will find examples which range from the strictly formal feng shui of ancient Chinese mansions (which have their own beauty and charm) through to much more modern examples of structures that have been designed according to discernable feng shui rules, or have unwittingly tapped into its manifest benefits.

Considerations of aesthetics, color and furnishings form part of feng shui. The marriage of sound feng shui principles and an aesthetic understanding of occupied spaces often produces the best balanced overall results. It is this carefully engineered yet seemingly effortless blend that this book sets out to explore.

Opposite: **From the living room, you can look straight through the bedroom to the dressing room and Jacuzzi at the rear of the photograph. Such a direct line of sight would not be considered beneficial, as it allows any arriving beneficial *ch'i* to rush straight through.**

BASIC PRINCIPLES OF FENG SHUI DESIGN

What is feng shui?

Feng shui is the art and science of changing the quality and flow of *ch'i* energy within a building, in order to benefit the health, wealth and happiness of the people living or working there.

What is *ch'i*?

Ch'i (also spelled *qi*) is the energy or life force or "breath" that flows through water, the earth and all living things. It is as subtle as radio waves, yet as concrete as a mountain stream. *Ch'i* is also found in buildings and the human body. In the body, *ch'i* may be affected by acupuncture techniques. In a building, *ch'i* may be modified by feng shui techniques. In both cases it is beneficial to have a steady flow, neither stagnating nor rushing rapidly, to obtain the greatest benefit.

What benefits does feng shui bring?

By harmonizing the *ch'i* energy in a building and its surrounding, the energy levels, efficiency and productivity of its occupants can be increased. Where sloth and muddle headedness may have existed previously, with the improvement of the *ch'i* flow and energy, the occupants will tend towards decisive actions and balanced emotions. This leads to, amongst other things, an increase in the number of business and relationship opportunities, which in turn results in improvements in health, wealth and happiness. In a more old fashioned way, you could say that improved feng shui in an apartment brings improved luck for its occupants, for what is luck apart from an increase in opportunities, and the energy and drive to grasp them?

How does it work?

Just as acupuncture can improve the energy flows along the meridians in the body, and just as martial arts training can toughen and strengthen the body, feng shui too, can improve the energy flows in the environment. *Ch'i* energy is not visible to an untrained person, but this does not mean it does not exist. Nobody has seen radio waves, but nobody doubts their existence, either.

What are the keys to feng shui analysis?

Feng shui analysis relies upon five things:
- landform
- alignment
- magnetic direction (as determined by a compass)
- timing (as measured by the Chinese calendar)
- changing *ch'i* cycles as mapped by:
  - the Trigrams of the I Ching
  - the energy represented by the five Chinese Elements and their cycles
  - the Lo Shu and Ho T'u squares
  - the nine Flying Stars (which are just fanciful names for specific energies)

The ability to judge and calculate the quality of *ch'i* in a building, and the knowledge of techniques which can be used to improve it, is the essence of the practice of feng shui. Let us now consider each of the keys to feng shui analysis in turn.

Landform

The oldest feng shui texts (dating back to at least 324 CE) are concerned with how a dwelling fits into its surrounding landscape. In fact the old name for feng shui was *ti li*, which is also currently used to mean "geography" in Chinese. The idea was that you needed to position your house in an area that was protected behind by a mountain or range of mountains, and enfolded on either side by a lower row of hills. Looking out from the front door of your new home, you should be able to see a lower open space in front (called a *ming tang* or "bright hall") that should be fronted by water (in the form of a pool, lake, river or even the sea) and ideally beyond that, a small rise. This positioning is often compared with an armchair, where the back represents the mountains, the arms are the hills on either side, and the small rise beyond the water is a footstool. This "armchair" configuration (see opposite page) will help to draw in and conserve the *ch'i* energy for the benefit of the house. The water acts as a boundary, and the *ming tang* provides room for the *ch'i* energy to accumulate. The "arm" hills protect the *ming tang* from strong winds that would otherwise disperse the *ch'i*. The best position for the house to be located in this configuration is called the *hsueh* or feng shui "it" spot. This is the spot where "the dragon and tiger couple" and is the place which a good feng shui master will locate for his client's home—the perfect configuration in a rural setting. In the city, although compromises must be made, the external configurations are still the most important considerations, as they bring the *ch'i* energy to your house in the first place.

Alignment

Such was the ideal configuration (not always facing due south, as some texts would suggest). A gently meandering river (or road) also helps bring and accumulate beneficial

Black Tortoise
Mountain
(back support)

Green Dragon Hill
(side protection)

White Tiger Hill
(side protection)

Bright Hall
(open space in
front of house)

Red Bird Hill
(footstool)

ch'i. In addition, there must be no alignments or large aggressive looking structures that "threaten" the peace of your new home. These include large buildings, long lines of telegraph poles and streets full of pillars or sharp objects pointed directly at a house. These are not beneficial, especially if they concentrate fast flowing *ch'i* energy towards the house door. *Ch'i* should always approach along a sinuous path, and not arrive rapidly by direct lines. *Ch'i* arriving too directly and rapidly is referred to as *sha ch'i*.

It is therefore important to look at the surrounding landscape to identify not only beneficial structures but also any non-beneficial features, and protect the house under consid-

eration from the non-beneficial features by placing suitable screens, fences or walls between the source of the *sha ch'i* and the house (particularly its doors and window). These are the basic considerations of landform feng shui, which deals with with the manipulation of visible *ch'i* paths.

Magnetic direction

Apart from the visual clues provided by the landscape, another aspect of feng shui also deals with invisible *ch'i* flows. This is Compass School feng shui. The main feng shui instrument used to identify *ch'i* flow is the Chinese compass or *lo p'an*. This instrument consists of a circular (Heaven)

will go through a cycle varying from strong and active to stagnant and non-beneficial. It is usual to identify the Period in which a house or building was constructed or "born." From the Period of birth, a feng shui practitioner can determine the future course of events, in broad terms, in that building. The most recent 20-year Periods are:

Period 1:   1864–1883
Period 2:   1884–1903
Period 3:   1904–1923
Period 4:   1924–1943
Period 5:   1944–1963
Period 6:   1964–1983
Period 7:   1984–2003
Period 8:   2004–2023
Period 9:   2024–2043

We have very recently passed from Period 7 to Period 8 (as of 4 February 2004) and this change will be felt in every house and building, with some moving into a period of prosperity and some moving out of such a period, depending upon their orientation. A lesser energy change then takes place each year.

Changing *ch'i* cycles

As feng shui is all about *ch'i*, we need to understand its vocabulary and ways of explaining and of categorizing the various types of energy, be they strong or weak, beneficial or otherwise, in any building or home. This vocabulary is founded primarily upon the nomenclature of Taoist cosmology, of which the most common terms are the terms for the five Elements or "phases."

The flow of *ch'i* in a house

The modern house (see opposite page) shows how *ch'i* flows along rivers or roads, enters the house through its front door, and then circulates in ever decreasing strength through the house, escaping finally through the rear door and to a lesser extent, through windows. It is preferable that *ch'i* meanders and flows in curved lines. Straight alignments are discouraged because *ch'i* flowing in straight lines for any distance will speed up and becomes harmful *sha ch'i*. Note that the entrance driveway to the house does not run straight from the road to the door, but is deliberately designed in an arc.

Internally, it is most important to ensure that this flow is not obstructed. The exception are the toilets, which are a source of *sha ch'i* and should be kept closed.

plate that rotates in a square (Earth) base. Its use in feng shui predates the use of the compass as a maritime device by hundreds of years.

The *lo p'an* has as many as 38 concentric rings, and is a complex visual compendium of feng shui rules. Its most basic use however, is to determine the direction from which *ch'i* arrives at the house, and hence the type of energy that affects a particular building or room in that building. The facing direction of the house (which is often the facing direction of its front door) is where most *ch'i* energy enters a house, so it is important to identify this direction by using the compass, in order to determine the type of energy that the building "inhales."

The *lo p'an* is also used to determine the bearing of surrounding natural and man-made features, particularly water features such as lakes, swimming pools and rivers. It is also used to check the direction of mountain peaks and buildings (which are the equivalents of mountains in a city). These alignments can then be screened off (if they are inauspicious) or enhanced (if they are beneficial), thus improving the energy balance of the home under consideration.

Timing

Feng shui divides time into periods, some as long as 180 years, during which the energy present in a particular house

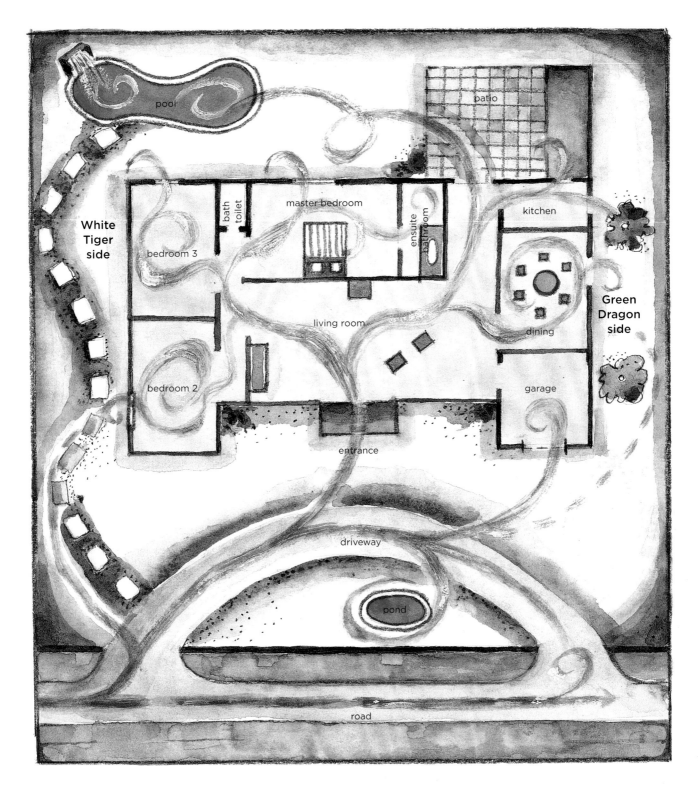

pool

White
Tiger
side

bedroom 3

bath
toilet

master bedroom

ensuite
bathroom

patio

kitchen

Green
Dragon
side

bedroom 2

living room

dining

garage

entrance

driveway

pond

road

Trigrams of the I Ching

Depending on their year of birth, each individual is assigned one of the eight Trigrams or *kua* numbers. This *kua* number will determine which for each person is the ideal facing direction for their house and for themselves. Part of feng shui practice consists of determining this personal Trigram and applying it to the positioning of furniture—particularly beds, study desks and favorite sitting chairs.

The Five Chinese Elements

The five Chinese Elements, Water, Fire, Earth, Wood and Metal are not Elements in the Western sense. They are more like energies rather than the hard physical substances that their names suggest. Part of feng shui practice consists of concentrating one Element or another in a particular part of a house or building. A very clear example is illustrated in the chapter on the former Daily Express building. This building was designed with ripple blue and black floors, to not only symbolize the element of water, but to actually accumulate the energy represented by the Chinese Element of Water. In feng shui thinking, the accumulation of the Water Element is linked with the accumulation of wealth, which partly explains why water features are such a common part of feng shui practice.

One of the most important things about the five Chinese Elements is that they produce (and destroy) each other in a strict sequence. The production sequence is Water -> Wood -> Fire -> Earth -> Metal -> Water. In this same building that has the Water floors, the surrounding walls and ceiling have been sculpted in metal, helping to reinforce the Chinese Element of Metal. From the above cycle, we know that Metal generates Water, so it becomes obvious that the designer was further strengthening the Water Element in this building, a building that did indeed create conspicuous wealth for its owners.

These elemental energies can be strengthened by the use of their corresponding physical elements. In the photograph of the Malaysian Airlines Golden Lounge at Heathrow airport in London (see page 15), you can see that although all the five Elements are present, with Earth represented (in the form of the large terracotta jars), Metal (in the water trays), Wood (in the form of growing plants) and less obviously Fire (in the form of strong lights), the emphasis is upon the Element of Water (especially in its function as an accumulator of prosperity).

Lo Shu and Ho T'u squares

The Lo Shu square consists of the first nine digits laid out in a square. It is used as a basic template applied to a house to determine the energies at play within its constituent rooms and also to decide where, for example, the best bedrooms for specific members of the family are. Its basic form is:

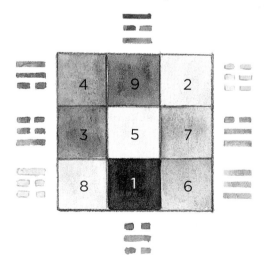

This template forms the basis for a form of feng shui analysis picturesquely called Flying Star analysis. This template is also used to track the changes and passage of energy in a house over time.

The Nine Flying Stars

These are not really stars. Rather, they are just fanciful names for nine specific energies or types of *ch'i*. By charting their movement inside a building over time, you can determine the sort of energies that are affecting the occupants and modify them accordingly. The Stars have names that are a combination of numbers and colors.

The beneficent Stars are:
1-white
6-white
8-white

the malevolent stars or negative energies are:
2-black
5-yellow

other variable energies are
3-green
4-green
7-red
9-purple

In some of the buildings discussed in this book I have shown the location of these energies in the building in order to explain how the changing feng shui has affected the building positively or negatively.

When analyzing the energies or *ch'i* in a house or building, you need first to determine which way it faces. This facing direction will often, but not always, be the direction faced by the main door. The reverse of this is the sitting direction that will often correspond with the back of the building. The facing direction will always be directly opposite the sitting direction. An S1 facing building for example, faces somewhere between 157.5 and 172.5 degrees, in other words, pretty close to due south at 180 degrees, but not quite. Precision is also required in feng shui measurement, just as in any other science.

Detailed Feng Shui Analysis

Wherever a building is analyzed in terms of Flying Star feng shui, the Stars are listed in the sequence: (Mountain Star) - (Base or Period Star) - (Water Star)

The Mountain Star affects people, relationships and health of the occupants. The Period Star relates to the time the building was built and therefore, the energies that were present then. The Water Star affects the wealth and material prosperity of the occupants. For example, 5-7-8 at the facing side means that the front part of the building has a Mountain Star of 5 (affecting the health and family of the residents negatively), a Period Star of 7 (meaning it was built between 1984 and 2004) and a Water Star of 8 (affecting the wealth luck of the occupants beneficially).

For readers who desire to understand and examine the science of feng shui in greater depth, I have included some specific feng shui analysis on some of the examples where it is particularly relevant. This analysis is based on Flying Star feng shui and more details of this system of feng shui can be found in one of my previous feng shui books, *Flying Star Feng Shui*. In this book, I have shown as many of the different aspects of feng shui as possible, with the emphasis of their application in a stylish manner.

Below: Huge earthenware jars continually overflowing with water symbolically represents wealth generation. It also provides a soothing background sound.

CLASSIC FENG SHUI

Traditional Chinese feng shui is concerned with feng shui as it was practiced in China in Imperial times and subsequently, in Chinese influenced areas like Singapore, Hong Kong, Malaysia and the Philippines. It is concerned with the flow of *ch'i* energy through the landscape. This energy is carried particularly strongly via water and through the "dragon veins" in mountain ranges. In fact the word for "landscape" in Chinese means mountain-water. Feng shui is a precision process that depends on finding these lines of energy in mountain ranges and in rivers and lakes, and ensuring that the most beneficial ones reach the house under consideration. Calculating the exact effect of these energies upon a particular house was the diagnostic part of traditional feng shui. Good *ch'i* was to be encouraged and inauspicious energies were to be blocked off or deflected. To do this, the practitioner noted the nearby mountains (or other building) and bodies of water and took their exact compass alignments from the building under consideration. Bodies of water included rivers and lakes right down to local drainage, and now, swimming pools. Water is particularly important, so careful plumbing and drainage was used to control its accumulation and dispersal to and from the home.

The facing direction of the building was also checked with the feng shui compass or *lo p'an*, as this affected the quality of *ch'i* reaching the building from the front. Alignments with other buildings were also taken into account. Only then would the feng shui master enter the house and look at the interior layout, mostly with an eye to the suitability of specific rooms for specific purposes, often using the birth dates of the occupants to determine their best bedrooms.

These energies fluctuated, grew and decayed over time. A building that has terrific feng shui now may not enjoy the same great feng shui forever. A building that has good feng shui for one individual, may not benefit another person. This calculation under Flying Star feng shui is an integral part of any feng shui consultation.

CHEONG FATT TZE MANSION
MANDARIN MANSION

From a feng shui point of view, this old Chinese mansion built in Penang between 1880 and 1889 is a wonderful example of classical late Ch'ing dynasty feng shui. The original owner Cheong Fatt Tze (1840–1916) was a self made man who rose from total poverty to the position of senior mandarin under the last Emperors of China. He was also ambassador for China under the emerging nationalist government, a multimillionaire and one of the first Chinese capitalists of the post-Imperial period. A measure of the man is that he was on his way to New York to negotiate a $10-million loan with Rockefeller at the time of his death. $10 million was an awful lot of money in 1916.

Never a man to do things by halves, Cheong Fatt Tze had a number of houses in China and Southeast Asia. This mansion in Penang housed several of his nine wives and was built with the assistance of some of the best feng shui experts of the period. Immediately noticeable from the front is the fact that the alignment of the mansion, and of its false front fence, is different from that of the road that it faces. This may have simply been done to square off the front of the property but more likely, it had a feng shui related reason. The mansion faces SE2, whilst the road faces SE3. As the feng shui at the date of its construction was as perfect as it could be made, this deliberate orientation of its facing direction was probably quite significant.

Architecturally, the mansion was built around one central courtyard open to the sky, in traditional Chinese style. It was then extended sideways in both directions to encompass a further four courtyards, making five courtyards in all, symbolizing the five Chinese Elements that lie behind Chinese cosmology, and feng shui theory and practice especially. With the central courtyard open to the elements, Heaven *ch'i* is able to come down to Earth, via Weather *ch'i* or rain, fertilizing and making prosperous the house in which it is collected and nurtured.

In practice, wind and rain enter through the sky opening into the courtyard where it is pooled (a few steps just below the main floor level). The water then drains as slowly as possible through torturous culverts under the floor, in order that the water and hence the *ch'i*, is retained in the building for as long as possible. The drains in fact often loop and double back (as they also do at roof level), before finally releasing the water into the gully that surrounds the whole house. The lowered center of the courtyard thus acts as a receptacle for the rain, which was then allowed to slowly run off through sub-floor drains, figuratively fertilizing the house

Left: The main courtyard is the heart of the house. The courtyard is not roofed over so here, the house receives wind and rain. A splendid wooden carved and gilded linen-fold style screen communicates between this area and the entrance hall. Such screens had the important function of separating the "bright hall" or *ming tang* which was the semi-public area immediately inside the main doors, from the more private and family areas around this courtyard and to the rear of the building.

Right: The main central door to the mansion is painted with golden calligraphy that says poetically "the *feng* dances and the dragon flies." Here *feng* means the Red Bird that is one of the four Celestial Animals, and is symbolic of the south. The dragon that flies is symbolic of the east. Taken together the two Celestial Animals indicate the SE, which is indeed the facing direction of the front door of the mansion, and the most auspicious facing direction for its owner.

Above: Soon after the central part of the house was constructed, two wings were added. Nearest is the Green Dragon wing, the strong *yang* male side, which is also where the main street gateway is located. The largest garden is also located on this side, where it supports the Green Dragon. The White Tiger or *yin* side of the house is less grand, in line with the idea that one should give prominence to the *yang* side. Where you find the opposite—a house with a stronger *yin* side—you often find that the wife rather than the husband is the one who "wears the trousers" in the family.

with its *ch'i* as it did so. Modern feng shui design, however, tends to forget that the arrangement of real water flow is more vital to the feng shui of a house than its furnishings, colors or furniture positioning.

A *chian* or bay, was the basic unit of Chinese house construction. The central section of the Mansion is three *chian* (bays) wide and two storeys high. Traditional Chinese buildings tended always to be an odd number of *chian* wide. For a small house, one *chian* wide was adequate, and is the pattern of the typical shop houses commonly found in both Singapore and Malaysia. When a larger residence was required it would never be two *chian* wide, but would go immediately to three *chian*. The feng shui reason for this is that odd numbers (1, 3, 5, 7 etc) were considered Heaven or *yang* numbers, whereas even numbers (2, 4, 6, 8, etc) were *yin* numbers.

The style of the mansion is eclectic, and it blends together the best of Chinese workmanship and design, with the best colonial products of the period. The courtyard flooring is of granite slabs and French tiles and is surrounded by Victorian Scottish cast-iron columns and railings—an interesting contrast with the gold-leaf Chinese carved timber filigree panels and painted *trompe l'oeil*

Left: One of the four side courtyards. A small fountain in the corner suggests that Water may be the appropriate Element of this courtyard.

Below: The lines of the *pa kua* or eight Trigrams have been punched into these metal door handles. This particular arrangement has *Ch'ien* or the Heaven Trigram at the top, and so they appear to be laid out in the Former Heaven Sequence. However closer inspection will show that the left and right (*Li* and *Kan*) Trigrams have been swapped. This is not a mistake, but an interesting reversal of the Water-Fire polarity derived from one of the feng shui formulas utilized in the mansion.

Far below: Above the front arcade is a similar balcony accessible only from Cheong Fatt Tze's private rooms. Here, he could command a view of the front garden, and perhaps more importantly, his shop houses on the other side of Leith Street.

beams and lime plastered decorative capitals. The staircases were built with gold coins buried at strategic points in order to help attract wealth into the mansion.

Although the perfect house "sitting" position for the Emperor was considered to be due north, the perfect house sitting position is different for different people. This position is determined by the Annual Flying Star at the year of their birth, or more simply, their *kua* number. Cheong Fatt Tze's birth in 1840 means that his *kua* number was 7. Hence the perfect alignment or *sheng ch'i* direction for him would be a house sitting at NW and facing SE. As you would have expected, the Mansion indeed sits to the NW and faces SE.

The colonnaded corridor alongside the side courtyards is illuminated with traditional red lanterns. These corridors lead to spiral staircases that are to be found at the back of the mansion, also made of Scottish ironwork. The feng shui caveat against using spiral staircases in a house seems to have only evolved in the 20th century, where their precipitous circular descent was thought to generate a sort of corkscrew *sha ch'i*. Cheong Fatt Tze's feng shui master obviously had no such reservations.

The mansion was built between 1880 and 1889 so its construction started in Period 1 and ended in Period 2. If the

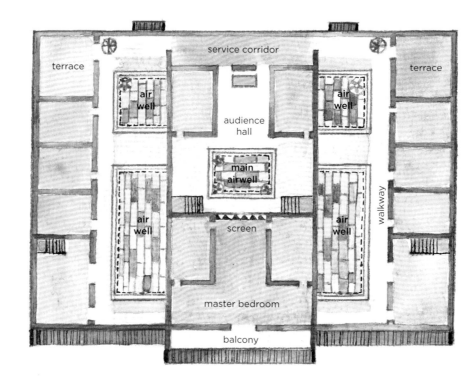

terrace

service corridor

air well

air well

audience hall

main airwell

air well

air well

screen

walkway

master bedroom

terrace

balcony

sitting NW2

added wing

added wing

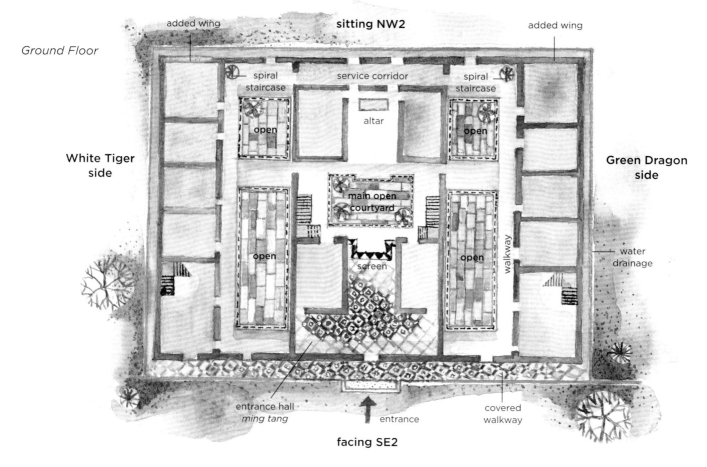

spiral staircase

service corridor

spiral staircase

open

altar

open

White Tiger side

Green Dragon side

open

main open courtyard

open

water drainage

screen

walkway

entrance hall *ming tang*

covered walkway

entrance

facing SE2

Plans: The Mansion faces SE2 and sits NW2, in line with the personal *kua* number 7 of its owner. The five open courtyards benefit its air and *ch'i* circulation. On the ground floor, the entrance hall acts as an interior *ming tang* which gathers *ch'i*. It is separated by a wooden screen from the central courtyard and the family quarters where the altar is located.

Period 1 NW2 Sitting direction		
4 7 3	3 8 2	7 4 6
8 3 7	2 9 1	5 6 4
6 5 5	**1 1** 9	9 2 8
Front door Facing Direction SE2		

Above, top: When it rained, the lowered centre of the courtyard would act as a receptacle for the rain, one of the five Weather *ch'i*.

Above: Flying Star charts are usually shown with the south at the top. However, so that the chart may be compared with the floor plans on the opposite page, I have reconfigured it with the facing direction (SE2) at the bottom. The two 1-white Stars at the front door opens the mansion to the maximum benefit for family, health and prosperity.

determining factor of which period the house was "born" in is the date the main roof ridge pole was put up, and that of the completion of the central block, then the mansion is most likely to have been considered a Period 1 house. However, if completion of the whole house was considered the house's "birth" time, then it is considered a Period 2 house (completion after February 1884). Both charts have very good Flying Star charts.

If the mansion was built in Period 2, then we can predict that its life cycle would have developed as follows. From its construction, its energy would have continued to rise till 1903, when its energies would have begun to level off and fall. By 1924 its energies would have died and would have remained so till 1983. In fact, the house fell into wrack and ruin during this time as it entered a period of *ssu ch'i* or torpid *ch'i*. This period was marked by the breaking up of the house into sub-tenancies and squats, indicative of this type of negative *ch'i*.

As soon as Period 7 arrived in 1984, the energies in the house revived. It was sold to its present owners in 1990, and the work of reconstruction begun. How do we know that? Period 7 (1984–2003) is under the auspices of the Element Metal and Metal produces or "feeds" Water, which is the Element that was present in Period 1 when the house was born. So, soon after the beginning of Period 7 the mansion was "fed," that is to say, restored. We can predict that these energies will continue to rise until the end of 2023, at which point they will again wane.

When analyzing this Flying Star chart we must remember that the time is the 1880s, when the 1-white and 2-black Stars were in ascendancy (1864–1884 for the 1-white Star, and 1884–1904 for the 2-black Star). In the 21st century, we are used to looking at the 2-black as a malevolent Star but the period 1884–1904 is in fact ruled by the 2-black Star, and thus, it is indeed most beneficial, and the bringer of great

Below: A view of the elaborate Scottish ironwork in the main courtyard.

Left: On the upper floor level, a balcony runs around the whole main courtyard, giving access to the rooms on that level, and allowing the occupants to benefit from the air circulation of the courtyard.

Opposite: On the upper floor looking from the rear of the building towards the front, you can see the balcony rails of the open courtyard. Beyond that is the wooden fanfold screen which marks off Cheong Fatt Tze's private rooms and bedrooms. From this position, Cheong Fatt Tze would have had a commanding view of the heart of the house. It is very possible that he used this hall as an audience chamber, sitting on a massive chair right at the point the photograph was taken from.

fertility (in terms of agriculture, children and trade) to this house. As such, for the duration of Cheong Fatt Tze's life the 2-black Star would have been very beneficial, only turning malefic later in the 20th century, when the mansion did in fact fall into disrepair and decrepitude. This decline of the fortunes of the mansion could have been easily predicted by the original feng shui Master who helped design it.

The Period 1 chart for the mansion is excellent. First it has both 1-white Stars (see page 23) at the front door, opening the mansion to the maximum benefit for family, health and prosperity. The third Star at the front door (the 9-purple Star) also considerably amplifies these benefits. This type of chart is called a Double Facing chart, because both the Stars of the Period are at the facing Palace.

In addition, the chart is a special chart, called a *he shih chu*—literally "Combination to Ten Configuration." When examining each Palace (or box) in the chart, you will see that in every case, two of the Stars add to ten. This type of chart is totally beneficial.

Ten is considered to be a number of completion. The Chinese character for ten is like an equal armed cross showing balance in all directions. It is interesting to note that the Chinese already had a decimal system of counting in the 14th century BC, during the Shang dynasty, some 2,300 years before the introduction of decimal arithmetic in Europe circa 976 AD and long before the decimal point was introduced to Europe by John Napier in 1617. Therefore, it is not surprising to find that ten is seen as a "completion number."

Cheong Fatt Tze certainly lived a full and complete life.

Right: At the left hand end is a *bas-relief* of a tiger which is symbolic of the White Tiger—the Celestial Animal of the *yin* side of the building.

Opposite: The two protective stone lions stand well out in front of the *kongsi*. On the roof are the elaborate dragons and dragon carp made in *chien nien* decoration work made from highly coloured porcelain.

KHOO KONGSI CLAN HOUSE
ANCESTOR FENG SHUI

Feng shui has a long history and the design minimalism of the 1980s and 1990s, is in stark contrast to the incredibly elaborate and detailed feng shui decoration as it was practiced a century ago. One of the best places to see such work is in the Chinese expatriate colonies in Southeast Asia, where craftsmen were imported by the hundreds from mainland China to work on the houses and clan houses of the newly arrived and often, very rich Chinese who had made their fortune in the great "south land."

Khoo Kongsi is the clan house of the Khoo family, who were immigrants from China during the 19th century. When it was built in Penang from 1904–6, it was subject to painstaking feng shui analysis. The reason for this is that just a few years earlier, a much larger and more impressive clan house had been built on the same site. However, before the ancestral tablets of the Khoo clan could be installed and the place officially opened, a mysterious fire burnt it to the ground on the eve of Chinese Lunar New Year. Only a few artefacts could be salvaged. The general opinion at the time was that the gods did not approve, or that the feng shui must have been incorrect, with too much emphasis being placed on the Fire Element. Hence in the planning of the new *kongsi*, much thought was given to the feng shui.

Although the detailed feng shui of a temple or a clan house is quite different from that of a home, the main principles are the same. The whole clan complex is located in the middle of a city block surrounded by houses (owned by the clan) that face outwards to the street. This gave it a marvellous defensive position and allowed for the quiet accumulation of *ch'i* within and hence, the accumulation of wealth.

The actual entrances though, are very insignificant archways that look just like very small and insignificant lanes between the houses. These then open out to a wide expansive square, the centre of which is protected by two guardian lions or *foo* dogs. They are very stylised and appear quite different from what might be recognised as a lion by a naturalist. Such lions are a feature of almost all traditional Chinese public buildings where protection from passing evil spirits is desired. Here, the lions are uncharacteristically placed in the middle of the square or *ming tang* in front of the *kongsi*, rather than tucked in either side of the front stairs or entrance as would be more usual.

These protective lions always come in pairs—one male and one female. In the case of the Khoo Kongsi lions, they are very clearly differentiated. The female is immediately recognisable, as she plays with a young cub held under her

Below: In the Central Hall on each wall are painted 18 guardian deities, making a total of 36. These are a mixture of heroes and divinities, but with the common function of protecting not just the Hall, but also the entire clan.

Left: The painted *men shen* or door guardians protect the main entrance of the Central Hall. These guardians are usually dressed in full military dress with weapons such as a sword, halberd or spear. They are designed to frighten away any *kuei* or ghosts, and demons. They have been a popular protection in China since at least 4th century BC.

Plan: A clan temple is a very special type of "house." The ancestors are represented by tiered plaques in the hall on the White Tiger *yin* side, whilst the earth gods are located on the Green Dragon *yang* side. The prayer pavilion is at a lower level than the main temple building, with a "royal way" or "spirit way" ramp at the front.

yin side

yang side

main altar

ancestors tablets

ancestors hall

men shen door guardians

hall of earth gods (brought from China)

tiger *bas-relief*

dragon *bas-relief*

dragon pillars

prayer pavilion

female lion

male lion

left paw, whilst the male lion holds a stone ribbon threaded with several old style square and round Chinese coins, symbolic of wealth. The male lion is on the right or *yang* side as you face the building. Indeed the Khoo clan has become, since the building of this clan house, the richest and best known Chinese clan in Penang, even owning plantations and a whole town (Bandar Baru, Ayer Itam) near Penang.

The *kongsi* faces into the courtyard. An interesting sidelight on its facing direction is that it faces away from the sea towards the mountain. Those familiar with Flying Star feng shui will know that the Mountain side symbolises the concerns of family and clan relationships, whilst the Water side is concerned with wealth.

From the courtyard, the stairs lead to the main terrace via an elevated Prayer Pavilion. Underneath the swallow-tailed roof of the Pavilion, motifs of the ubiquitous three-legged toad—which symbolises the acquisition of wealth—are depicted in almost psychedelic blues and red. On the next level is the main terrace, with the Ancestral Hall to the left. This of course is the *yin* side, and the dead are *yin* compared to their *yang* living descendants. In this hall are kept the rows of tablets (one row per generation) that represent the earliest generations of the Khoo clan in Penang. At either end of the top terrace are two of the four Celestial Animals used

Right: At the east end is a *bas-relief* of two dragons which are symbolic of the Green Dragon—the Celestial Animal of the *yang* side of the building.

Opposite: The roof of the long balcony is supported by granite pillars which have been carved in deep relief with dragons and other figures.

Above: The two guardian lions protect the center of the court-yard. The female lion, is on the *yin* side in the foreground of the photograph.

in feng shui to mark the left and the right side of the property. Facing the *kongsi*, the left hand (or *yin*) end of the terrace is a *bas-relief* of a tiger (symbolic of the west) whilst the right hand (or *yang*) end is the figure of the dragon (in fact, two of them here) symbolic of the east.

There is often confusion about the meaning of the four Celestial Animals, as they are usually attributed to the four cardinal directions: the Green Dragon (east), the White Tiger (west), the Black Tortoise and Snake (north) and the Red Bird sometimes wrongly described as a phoenix (south). These directions apply to the perfect Imperial temple that faces due south, but in the context of other homes or temples, the four Celestial Animals mark out the directions relative to the way that a building faces. So (facing the building), the Green Dragon is on the (*yang*) right side, the White Tiger is on the (*yin*) left side, the Black Tortoise and Snake are behind, whilst the Red Bird is in front facing the open courtyard.

In the center of the terrace is the Central Hall with side-wall murals depicting 36 protective gods and guards. To the right of the terrace (on the *yang* or active side) is a side temple for Hock Teik, the god of prosperity. It contains the local gods of the clan brought with them from Amoy (Xiamen) in Fujian province in China and these represent the earth and prosperity transplanted from their original ancestral home. Prosperity is seen as more than just wealth. This god is related to T'u Ti, the god of the earth in China, suggesting agricultural prosperity and fertility.

SENTA SAUJANA
CLOSE TO THE EARTH

Senta Saujana is situated in the jungle periphery on the top of a natural landform saddle. The name of this house, Senta Saujana, means "as far as the eyes can see," and is an indication of its elevated positioning. This is a classical example of traditional Malay "feng shui" in action. This house (despite its appearance) was only built 15 years ago, but is constructed according to traditional Malay principles.

Malay feng shui is concerned with the relationship of the house with both its surrounding landscape and with nearby residents, but is more intimately connected with ceremony and ritual than Chinese feng shui. The Malay equivalent of feng shui is very much concerned with the preparations of a place before building begins, and uses the services of a *bomoh*, or local magician to make the new house acceptable

to the spirits of the land. The *bomoh* is often called upon to secure love or cure illness, and his practices predate the introduction of Islam into Malaysia.

When someone decides to settle in an area, they will carefully level an area and mark out the limits of their house and compound after buying the land. Rather like the old English practice of beating the bounds, the new owner or his *bomoh*, or both, will walk round the perimeter marking it, making if you like, a perimeter against hostile influences of this world or the other. If the newcomer comes from a different area, he will then take some earth brought from his ancestral home, and enclosing it in a male coconut shell, bury it with appropriate ritual in the soil of his new compound. This establishes a link between his ancestors and his

Plan: The feng shui of the main hall is protected from *sha ch'i* by a screen. Separate buildings house the sleeping and eating functions, and are connected to the main building by covered bridges.

Right: The whole house is raised on wooden pillars set into stone supports, which in turn rest on a concrete platform. Around this runs the water drain and roof water simply runs off the eaves into the vicinity of this drain.

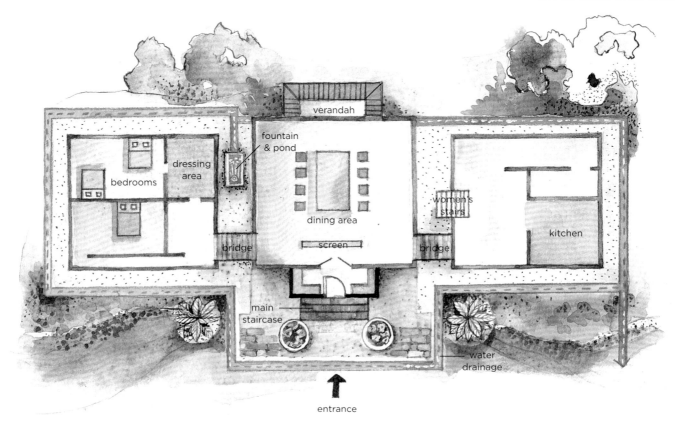

Right: The gate at the top of the entrance stairs separates the public area from the porch, a division that is as much practical as symbolic of the transition from public space to the space reserved for friends and family. The tray contains betel, shavings of the areca nut for use whilst talking. Through the entrance, is the main family and dining areas, protected by yet another wooden screen from the incursion of *sha ch'i,* or maybe just the stares of the curious.

Far left: Windchimes hang at the corner of one of the verandas. Such windchimes are sometimes thought to attract spirits.

Left: An old flour-grinding mill-stone does service as a fountain.

new abode. A party will then be held to which he invites all his new neighbours, so that they can meet him and his family and at the same time, acknowledge that this piece of land now belongs to him and his family.

It is like the bedding down of the roots of a transplanted plant to ensure it will flourish in new earth. Reverence for the earth and the land is strongly inherent in these rituals. Next, the base of the main pillar of the house will be prepared and at its top, three different colored cloths will be placed before the main crossbeam or ridgepole is put into position. This is akin to Chinese feng shui where the placement of the ridgepole coincides with the placement of protective talismans and is deemed the most significant moment. It is believed that the time of setting the ridgepole into position is the "birth date" of the house.

This also relates to the feng shui practice of re-setting the "birth period" or Earth Base of a house by lifting the roof (or in reality, replacing the ridgepole). Often, the main vertical pillar of a Malay house is not in the center, but off to the right hand of the center (looking out) because ideally, the central area should be kept an open space.

This particular traditional Malay house is really three houses. The central house is connected by covered walkways with two side houses, emphasising the division of function which is an overriding concern of Malay house construction and also that of Chinese feng shui. The normal shape of a classical Malay house is long and narrow, with public areas at the front. These are followed by eating, then living areas, with cooking areas at the back. Sleeping quarters will often be to either side. In this example, (looking outwards) the kitchen plus the women's entrance is located on the left or Green Dragon side, whilst the quieter *yin* sleeping quarters are located on the right or White Tiger side.

Just underneath the house is a generous and cool entertaining area, without walls, but with the same floor area as the whole house. It serves to effectively double the size of the house.

A water feature is placed to the rear of the house on the White Tiger side. Traditionally, this would have been considered as giving an emphasis to the *yin* or feminine side of the house.

The eaves do not have gutters. Instead, the rainwater runs off the roof into a ground drain that catches the overflow from the eaves and runs parallel to the outline of the entire house. From a feng shui perspective it is important to plan the exit direction of this water drain, although in this case, the water is simply routed to a convenient slope beyond the confines of the house's immediate area. Chinese feng shui pays much more attention to the direction of collection and distribution of water runoff round a house, sometimes making it consciously into a Water Dragon. The principles behind the creation of a Water Dragon are quite complex, but the basic principle is that the source of water should come from a beneficial direction, whilst the exit point of the water should be fixed in a non-beneficial direction, to drain those energies, or alternatively, be completely hidden so as not to drain any energies. A *lo p'an* or Chinese compass, is used for such measurements.

WIND HOUSE
DESIGN

The wind, or *feng*, is an integral yet often-neglected aspect of feng shui. It is a known fact that rushing water is not conducive to good *ch'i* flow. Similarly, positioning a house on top of a windy ridge does not usually bring feng shui benefits either. The traditional "armchair" configuration of land-form feng shui, with its backing mountain and two arms of hills on either side, ensures that the site is well protected from savage winds. In the context of a house, it is best to avoid isolated buildings built high on ridges where beneficial *ch'i* will be blown aside.

At the opposite extreme, stagnant air or *ssu ch'i*, is not conducive either to health or good feng shui either. The parallel with water is that you will never find a thriving metropolis located either on fast flowing rapids or in a swamp. These extremes are obvious examples.

Just as water must not be stagnant, it must also be ensured that air and the *ch'i* it brings with it, circulates through the house reaching all rooms, leaving no areas of stagnant air or stale condensation. These days, air-conditioning is often seen as the answer particularly in offices. But the re-circulation of reused and denatured air is not the best way to circulate beneficial *ch'i* that relies upon fresh air to carry it. But how do you control the flow of air in a stylish fashion in an ordinary home? In the following pages we look at three dwellings that, although built recently, have avoided the worst excesses of artificiality and air-conditioning. They have gone instead for a natural play of fresh air through the house, with a flow that can be regulated by ingenious devices such as the "feng shui window." This invention by architect Jimmy Lim, is effectively a vertical cylinder window that turns to admit an easily regulated amount of breeze without slamming shut.

You will not see the latter in a traditional feng shui manual, but its operation is certainly close to the spirit of feng shui. In tropical regions, the play of air through the building is also important from a cooling point of view.

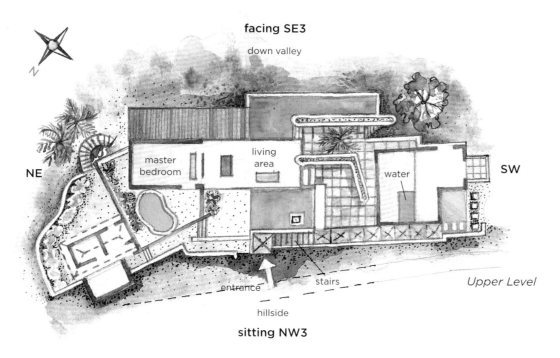

facing SE3

down valley

N

NE

master
bedroom

living
area

water

SW

entrance

stairs

Upper Level

hillside

sitting NW3

Below: The front of Bayugita is fringed by a long pool, into which flows a spectacular sheet waterfall.

Right: The main living area of Bayugita is protected, rather strangely, by two ferocious wooden hogs. These are an interesting and witty variation on the use of Chinese lions or *foo* dogs as door guardians. To the right is the balcony with a magnificent view down the ravine, whilst to the left is an elaborate lotus pool.

Plan: This villa is built at different levels descending the hillside, with a long lap pool on the facing side. It is "supported" on the sitting side (NW3) by the hillside, which is where the entrance is also located. This is an example of a structure where the position of the entrance door and the facing direction are definitely not the same.

BAYUGITA
SONG OF THE WIND

Named after one of the Elements, this villa is called Bayu-gita. *Bayu* is the element of air and the décor and color palette of Bayugita follow the dictates of its element. The Balinese color correspondences attribute blue and white to air, and much of the furnishings in this villa consistently repeat this color scheme. Wind is not one of the five traditional Chinese Elements, but is nevertheless an important part of feng shui.

Located at Begawan Giri in Bali, Bayugita is carefully fitted into the rainforest, observing the contours of the land, and the natural fall of water. This villa is furnished with golden teak paneling, carved Batavia furniture and woven coconut ceilings. It has a slightly colonial flavor, reflected in the furnishings that include items made of terrazzo, porcelain and brass, like antique Victorian washbasins, and a copy of a Dutch colonial bed. Chinese influence can be seen in the fine medicine chests.

The most powerful entity present is the surrounding rainforest and its deep ravines that are filled with rushing water, and inhabited by spirits that modern man has long since forgotten. It is not unusual to see the local practice of appeasing such spirits with offerings of flowers and food. "Spirit walls" are also designed at entrances to prevent their casual incursion, following feng shui principles.

Left: A very necessary conical mosquito net is draped over a four-poster bed. Although it is often said that you should not sleep with something overhanging you, this more realistically applies to heavy picture frames or counter-balanced shelves rather than light and necessary mosquito nets. The perfection of the polished floors is relieved by several thick pile carpets.

Below: The lotus pond with pottery jar, plants and a carving which reflects the eddying of air.

PANGKOR LAUT PRIVATE ESTATE
FAR PAVILIONS

Pangkor Laut private estate is a handful of very private and self-contained pavilions grouped and focussed on several private beaches on Pangkor Laut island, and quite separate from the better known spa and sea villas shown on this page. Each estate has been created with its own facilities, be it bedroom, dining room, or reading room in its own dedicated pavilion, with paths interconnecting them. In good weather, nothing could be more delightful or peaceful.

The feng shui of this arrangement is not one of many rooms in a house, but that of separate pavilions dedicated to different functions, each of which needs to be considered separately. For example, the bedroom and spa bathroom are one unit at some distance from the dining and kitchen area, which in turn is some distance from the pavilion that might be considered the living room.

The idea of a home built as a collection of separate pavilions probably originated in Bali where the accommodating climate, and the Balinese regard for ritual purity, which dictates the clear separation of different household functions, make this a desirable format. Some of this thinking about ritual purity also persists in Chinese (or indeed Welsh) architectural rules about toilets, where traditionally such functions (even in a very grand mansion) would have been deliberately located in a separate structure away from the main house.

This is also part of the background to various feng shui prohibitions concerning the "wet rooms" of a house (the bathroom, toilet and kitchen) where "ritual purity" translates practically to keeping foul water and hence *ssu ch'i*, away from the more important functions of the house, such as bedrooms and dining rooms. The modern feng shui adaption of this is to try and have these wet rooms located in those parts of the house that do not have beneficial feng shui energies, in an effort to "drain" them. In other words, positive functions like eating and sleeping should be located in positive areas, as determined by feng shui principles, whilst negative areas should be occupied by wet rooms, store rooms or guest bedrooms.

Left: Some of the the villas in the public area of Pangkor Laut are built on hills that enfold the site like the classical feng shui "armchair" formation. This beneficial configuration is further improved by the presence of a round frog pool positioned at the focus point on the flat land directly in front of the villas.

Opposite: The stilted sea villas pick their way between huge sea washed boulders scattered along the shore.

dining balé

lounge balé

pool

bedroom

bath/pool

sea

Below left: The dining pavilion is built into the landscape, with its steps accommodating the roots of an old and leaning tree. The appreciation and even reverence for trees, especially very old or characterful trees, is a universal phenomenon in Southeast Asia. This extends well beyond the Bodhi tree of Buddhism. Many Chinese temples have venerated "feng shui trees" and in Bali, Thailand and India, it is common to see trees dressed with elaborate cloths or sashes, with an offering or two to the tree spirit placed in front of them.

Below right: Inside the dining pavilion, with a full-length view on three sides of the pavilion, the connection with the natural surroundings is greatly enhanced.

Plan: Spread out in a series of pavilions by the seashore, the focus of this villa is on water, with its sleeping quarters embraced by the pool, and the dining balé facing the sea. The pavilions are deliberately connected by curved rather than straight paths to prevent the generation of *sha ch'i* by straight alignments. Each balé is self-contained.

Above: A traditional humpbacked bridge connects one of the minor pavilions. It is important that the ends of the bridge do not point directly at a pavilion. Bridges are always strong generators of *sha ch'i* which gains additional momentum as it crosses water.

Below: A small balé, open to the air and covered from the rain, is ideal for reading or just dreaming. It stands invitingly off to one side, surrounded by rainforest and is insulated from the earth on a stone pediment and four stone pillar rests.

Right: Inside the bedroom pavilion, showing the *alang alang* roof. The bed backs on to a window containing stone statues, which would normally be considered a bad idea, because the sleeper is given no "support" and is also threatened from behind.

Left: Adjoining the bedroom is the ensuite spa bathroom, with its view of the garden outside. The bath area does not open directly onto the bedroom, which would not be good feng shui. By being open to the air, the spa is not an integral part of the bedroom pavilion, and so has little effect on its feng shui.

Right: A smaller informal pavilion provides a perspective on the bedroom pavilion across the pool which embraces it like a sinuous Water Dragon.

Below right: Inside the bedroom.

JIMMY LIM RESIDENCE
A HOUSE WITHOUT WALLS

Above: Facing the door is a large earthenware receptacle. The pairs of Mandarin ducks—symbols of faithfulness and marital happiness—surmount it, whilst symbols of fertility in the form of fruits and coconuts are placed nearby.

Opposite: The main entrance is through a pair of classic Chinese double doors with two small guardians. The bulk of the cantilevered swimming pool looms on the right, and the first of many flights of roofing fantasy flutter above. The entrance doors are tilted to face SE. This is a change from the original due east orientation of the original doors of the basic house.

Jimmy Lim is a Kuala Lumpur based architect who specializes in tropical houses, and who has never felt the pressing need to design regular box-like enclosed houses. For Jimmy, designing as he does for tropical living, the ideal is a house without walls—a house in which the cooling is derived not from artificial air-conditioning, but from the action of every passing breeze. A house where the natural breath of nature, or *ch'i*, is allowed to enter at will.

Such a concept is quite traditional in terms of Chinese house building. Although traditional Chinese buildings always had walls, these were not the first things built, and often, not the most important part of a building either. Pre-modern Chinese houses and temples were built on platforms of stone, brick or rammed earth. On such a platform were planted load-bearing pillars that would then support a wide-eaved roof that was put up before any walls. Only after the roof was in place were the non-load bearing walls filled in between or around the pillars to create the rooms. From this, we can see that the emphasis in old Chinese feng shui manuals on changing the function of a room or altering the position of walls was quite practical in a way that Western-built houses, with their fixed concrete and brick load-bearing walls, can never achieve.

This is significant from a feng shui point of view: the installation of the roof ridgepole is considered the point when the building becomes a house, when Heaven *ch'i* (*t'ien ch'i*) is separated from Earth *ch'i* (*ti ch'i*) to make a space for Human *ch'i* (*ren ch'i*). Sometimes, establishing the time of this event is crucial in a feng shui calculation.

Jimmy Lim takes this traditional construction method a bit further by questioning the need for walls. Some architects, like those in Bali, happily construct balé which are roofed platforms open on at least three sides. In his own home, Jimmy Lim has experimented widely with adaptable walls, and sometimes, no walls at all.

Jimmy acquired his house, originally a basic typical square house in a suburb of Kuala Lumpur in 1976. Since then he has been embellishing it, like some modern day tower of winds, and his attention to the movement of wind through the walls is perhaps unparalleled by any other modern architect. Wall sections made of canvas flap upwards or downwards to dramatically change the flow of air, whilst roof panels open to the heavens as required, to increase or decrease ventilation.

The house is a sort of functional outdoors. Jimmy describes it as "a house that allows you to control your own destiny," and in the sense that it allows you to open walls,

Below right: Just inside the main doors, one of a pair of gilded wooden water buffalos greets visitors, a change from the traditional Chinese lions. Their mute wooden mouths are stuffed with red cloth, to stop them "eating" the beneficial *ch'i* that flows through the main entrance. Next to the main door, a concertina panel is folded back to admit more air. It is important to have a clear path for the *ch'i* to enter a building.

Opposite: The main sitting room is the heart of the house, and an eclectic mix of traditional dark wood Chinese furniture with a few more modern touches. This is not what you might expect to find in a building where the latest ideas in architecture are being tried out. It helps demonstrate that Jimmy's innovations come from a very traditional basis. The ubiquitous pairs of Mandarin ducks find expression in a large pair in the foreground.

or windows that previously appeared to be walls, or to change the function of a room, so it is. There is also a further layer of meaning to this statement in that by changing the pattern of air, and hence the *ch'i* movement, he changes the feng shui of the house.

With all this free flowing air, bats have taken to roosting in the house, bringing with them, luck. The word for bats, or *fu*, shares the same pronunciation as *fu* or luck in Chinese, and bats have therefore become recognized by the Chinese as a symbol of luck. Stylized bats can be seen in Chinese art and architecture from the patterns on common rice bowls to motifs in major temples.

Each of the many wooden decks in the house are linked via gravity defying flights of wooden steps, which sometimes rise like the pitch of the roof, only to fall again before reaching their appointed destination, in a pattern which is as intricate and perplexing as an Escher print. One purpose of this is to remove the importance of walls, and also that of the usual grid-like connection of rooms, instead replacing them with a raft of interconnected platforms, apparently free floating rooms, and processional ways suspended in three dimensional space.

What also makes the house fascinating is the combination of bright and airy spaces and host of traditional Chinese feng shui devices. The first of these juxtapositions is apparent upon reaching the front door. To the right is the massive brutalist raw concrete of the bottom of the swimming pool suspended in the air above head level. To the left are a pair of delicate gilded traditional Chinese wooden screen doors—beautifully carved with hand adjustable vertical ventilation slats in the best traditional form—which are the main entrance of the house.

Such an entrance should prepare you for what is inside... but it does not. While parts of the house are at the cutting edge of architectural experimentation, many of its furnishings are deeply traditional at the same time, from the black wood Ch'ing dynasty style chairs to the elaborate red and gold calligraphy, framed and hung high in the atrium.

Mandarin ducks, symbolic of lifetime affection, loyalty and marital happiness abound.

Left: The original east-facing door of the old house now opens into the garage, and does not condition the feng shui of the house anymore. As Jimmy was born in 1944, this makes 2 his birth *kua*. For him the best "sitting" directions would be NE, or NW if he aims to strengthen his relationship and family ties. Therefore it is not surprising that his main entrance door in fact faces SE.

Below: Framed calligraphy implying "success" or "fortune," is present not just as a pious hope but as a positive declaration designed to encourage its imminent arrival.

Plan: Like a "tower of winds," this four storey home can be opened to the air at any level, with walls that can be moved or even rolled up, thus changing the input of *feng*, or wind. The focus of the house is the open atrium (to the right side of the plan) that reaches through all the floors to the roof.

First Level

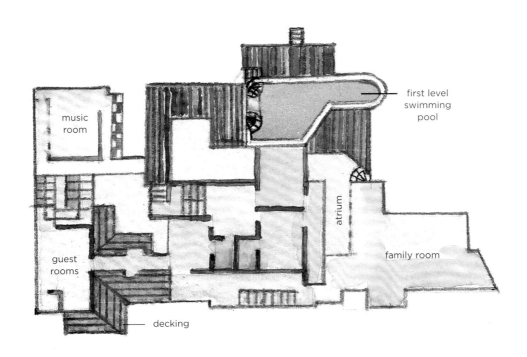

music room

first level swimming pool

atrium

guest rooms

family room

decking

Ground Level

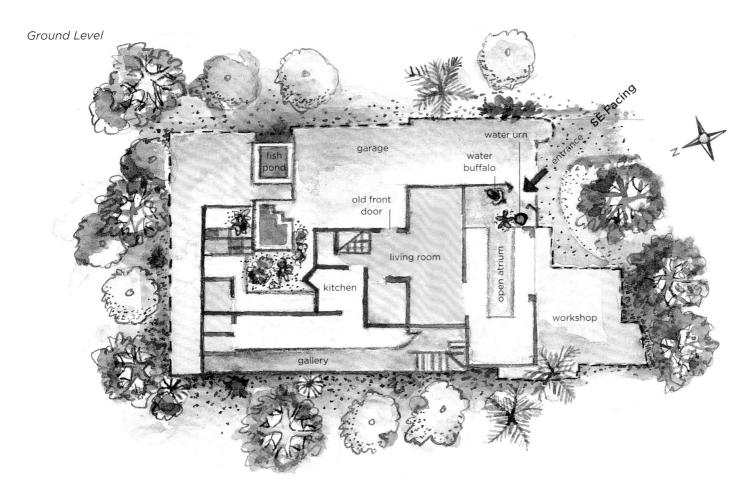

SE Facing

fish pond

garage

water urn

water buffalo

entrance

old front door

living room

open atrium

kitchen

workshop

gallery

N

WATER HOUSE DESIGN

Shui or water, is not only essential for life, but is also essential for good feng shui. Water carries *ch'i* energy, so its positioning must always be carefully considered. The ideal landform configuration, as we have seen, places water in front, and mountains behind an ideal site.

Traditional Chinese mansions were often set into a landscape where elaborate rivers or lakes with many branches embraced the house, helping to draw in and accumulate beneficial *ch'i*. This does not mean that every house should have a pond in front of it, but the correct placement of water in the grounds around a house can have a powerful effect on its feng shui, and the consequent luck of its owners.

Water can be used as a pool, a fountain, or if indoors, an aquarium or interior fountain in order to enhance some benevolent energies or "drown" other less desirable ones. Even apartments can have appropriate water features placed in the correct position in their living room or balcony.

The key considerations are that the water should be active, proportionate to the building, and not stagnant. In fact, too much water can be overwhelming. A classic example of this is where the owners of a house build a large swimming pool disproportionately close to their house, then find that they have overwhelmed some part of their life or luck. Big is not always best. In fact the guidelines of good design should naturally help to check the urge to construct something out of proportion with its surroundings. Both design and feng shui rely upon balance and harmony to achieve their ends.

It is often said that it is important to keep the toilet lid or door closed for good feng shui. This is no more than the desire to prevent stagnant water from influencing the feng shui of your house. In Flying Star feng shui, it is the Water Stars that govern wealth. So, stimulating the current or next Period Stars (8 and 9) with physical water will provide a simple but effective boost to your prosperity.

VILLA HUTAN DATAI
CLUSTER PAVILIONS

Villa Hutan Datai is built on a steep slope looking down towards Datai Bay on the island of Langkawi. Its positioning is good landform feng shui, with the higher slope behind the villa, and water in the foreground. The only thing missing are the enfolding hills either side of the site, and perhaps the slope is a little too steep to qualify as a classical "armchair" landform formation. Water in the foreground is key to the feng shui of this home, and the villa is focused around two bodies of water: in the foreground it is focused around the swimming pool, and beyond that it faces the sea.

The swimming pool has two corner fountains "feeding" it with water. It is important for feng shui purposes, to make sure that the point where the water enters the pool (and also where it exits) is located in the correct sector.

Right: The villa in perspective, showing how its various pavilions are grouped around the central swimming pool.

Below: Lush vegetation reflects both the climate and the intrinsic energy of the villa.

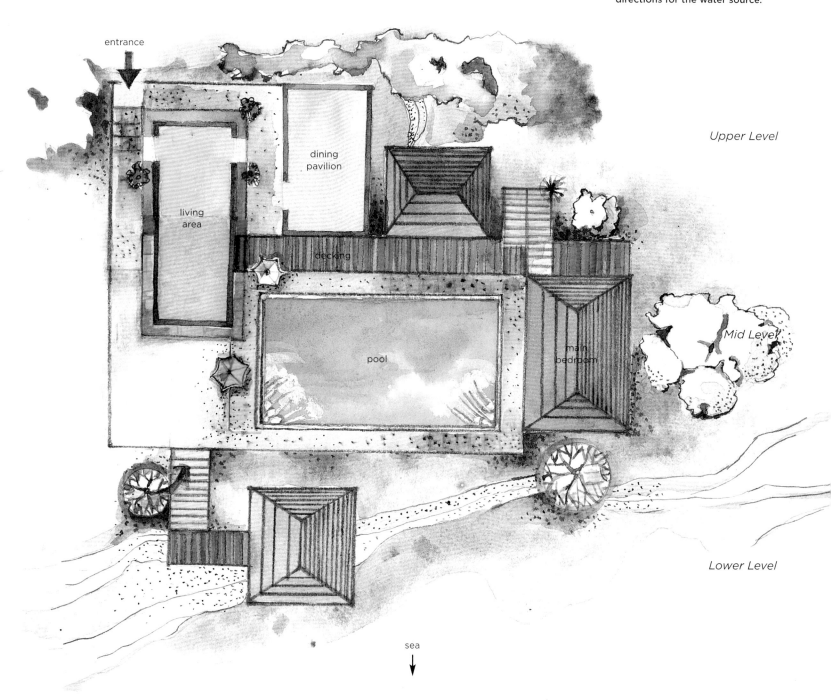

Plan: This villa faces the sea and the north and has its living, dining and bedroom pavilions grouped about its pool. This provides good form feng shui. Here, the water for the pool originates in its NE and NW corners. These directions are normally chosen with reference to the feng shui of the villa so as to ensure they are beneficial directions for the water source.

N

entrance

Upper Level

dining pavilion

living area

decking

Mid Level

pool

main bedroom

Lower Level

sea

The living area is by contrast backed by a shallow moat on three sides. Water behind a building is however, contrary to the usual feng shui practice, and leaves this particular room "unsupported" in a feng shui sense.

The rest of the villa consists of a number of separate free standing rooms or pavilions for different functions, interconnected by walkways. Each room therefore must have its feng shui also assessed separately. The main bedroom pavilion is located on the left hand side facing out from the villa, giving the whole complex a much stronger *yang* side, and this is reflected in the occupation of its racing driver owner.

Above: Several small islands out in the bay are framed by the balcony and surrounding trees.

Left: Interconnecting stairs and walkways unify the various pavilions into a whole.

Left: The dining room is decorated with many beautiful Chinese antiques that introduce balancing *yin* elements in opposition to the bright *yang* sun that enters through floor-to-ceiling windows.

Below: Modern paintings of antique subjects, like this painting of an antique Chinese throne being clambered upon by a Pu Yi figure (reminiscent of a scene out of *The Last Emperor*), helps unite the ultra modern room with its antique Chinese furniture.

Right: The living room or lounge pavilion is surrounded with an embracing moat on its mountain (rear) side, and faces out to sea. This pavilion is embraced by small trees on both sides, and behind, which help shade the room. The expanse of glass windows would otherwise be intolerably hot and *yang*. Empty earthenware jars are a feature of this room and are located in its NW corner. Like gourds, these traditionally absorb negative energy. Also the Element Earth that they represent, pro-duces the Element Metal which is appropriate to the NW corner of the room. In front of the jars are a couple of antique prayer scroll containers, invoking a different kind of protection.

VILLA TIRTA-ENING
CLEAR WATER

Although Hinduism is the nominal religion in Bali, the Balinese call their religion *Agama Tirta* (literally the "Science of the Holy Water"). It is an interpretation of Hinduism that includes ideas that may have been imported from China, such as the importance of the cardinal directions and that of water, both of which relate directly to feng shui. This villa backs into the hill, facing a ravine chasm and opposing a ridge on the other side. As water (or *tirta*) is its theme, it is appropriate that even before you enter the villa, you have to pass terraced lotus ponds set into the hill behind it.

Tirta's pavilions are made of 150-year old Javanese teak. The main living pavilion, shingle roofed and constructed of yellow rock and teak, appears to float on the water of its surrounding moat. Although it is not considered good feng shui to build over water, but as the theme of the villa is water or *apas*, it seems very natural. The villa looks over another horizon pool to the ravine below, which descends to the fast flowing Ayung River, just glimpsed between the trees.

The villa faces SE and sits in the NW sector. Anyone with a birth year *kua* of 7, and hence with their *sheng ch'i* located in the NW, should feel completely at home in this villa.

Looking out towards the ravine, the Green Dragon side is on the left hand. The pavilion on this side contains the deluxe suite, whilst the master suite is on the White Tiger or right side.

The feng shui of the bathroom is interesting. Normally the "wet rooms" in a home have an important part to play in its feng shui, as water both brings and carries away *ch'i*. The bathroom in Tirta is completely external to the villa. It consists of a platform suspended above the water of a private pool, and does not affect the feng shui in the usual way. Adjoining this platform is a unique stone bath, which combines both Earth and Water as it is carved out of a single six-ton boulder that was retrieved with great effort from the floor of the ravine. To bath in such a bath tub makes you very much feel at home with the water, the rocks, and nature.

Left: The main entrance to Begawan Giri, the complex which contains Tirta-Ening.

Opposite: The main pool is located on the facing side of the villa (showing part of the deluxe suite) on the Green Dragon side and the master bedroom on the White Tiger side (behind the photograph), which is exactly how well-balanced Form feng shui should be, with the *yang* of the dragon in slight ascendancy over the *yin* of the tiger.

Left: The gateway to the northern pavilion. Note the moss covered jar immediately inside the door, designed to trap *sha ch'i*.

Right: The main living area, which is the heart of the house, is floored in teak and central to the whole villa. It has been built with eight massive wooden posts supporting a high pitched overhanging roof, to protect the living area from tropical rain. Walls have not been filled in, allowing for a free flow of *ch'i*.

Plan: This villa consists of a stronger Green Dragon or *yang* side balanced against a less obtrusive White Tiger or *yin* side—the ideal balance. The pool located on its facing side is the key feng shui feature. The pool on its sitting side is architecturally interesting, but weakening from a feng shui point of view.

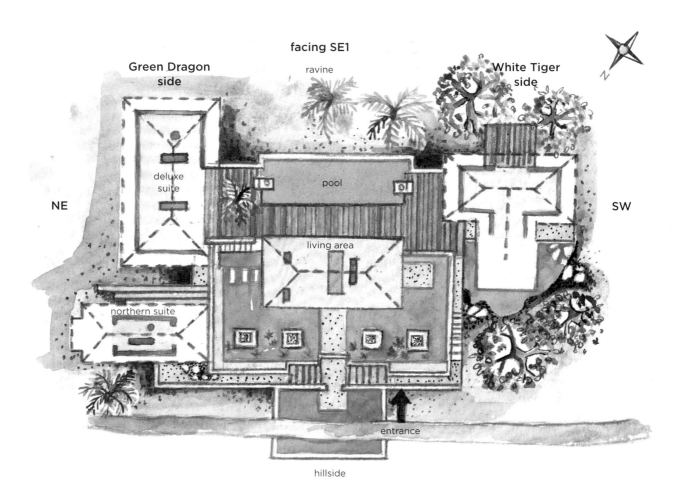

facing SE1

ravine

Green Dragon side

White Tiger side

NE

deluxe suite

pool

living area

northern suite

SW

entrance

hillside

sitting NW1

Below left: A Chinese altar table with flowers and a very free form example of Zen calligraphy forms part of the decoration of this room.

Below right: Where once the local Balinese would have bathed in the river at the bottom of the ravine, now, not just the water but also the rocks are brought up for the convenience of guests.

Right: The master bedroom ensuite bathroom platform, surrounded by water, showing the six-ton carved single stone bath, the balé and Jacuzzi in the background.

Left: The platform bed in the deluxe suite with free form calligraphy on the wall behind, plus the inevitable mosquito nets.

CHEF WAN'S COUNTRY ESTATE
SECRET RETREAT

Though better known for the pace of his cookery presentation on TV, Chef Wan also has a more reflective side. Far from the rush and bustle of Kuala Lumpur, he has a serene country villa hideaway on the other side of the peninsular. Here, water plays an important part in the form of an external fountain with three streams flowing into large earthenware jars set in a rectangular pool.

The main feature in his living room is the large window that opens directly onto the garden, bringing the outside in. His furniture is an eclectic blend of contrasting colors, a pleasing blend of *yin* and *yang*.

A decorative antique mirror helps to lighten the adjacent hallway. Special mirrors set into an octagonal surround inscribed with the eight *kua* or Trigrams (in the Former Heaven sequence) are often used to deflect the *sha ch'i* caused by straight alignments, particularly if these point at a main doorway. The use of ordinary mirrors in feng shui is more controversial, but some masters consider them able to reflect *ch'i* because of their watery associations. The use of mirrors (particularly polished metal mirrors) goes back a long way in China, so one should not dismiss their benefit in brightening up a space by introducing more *yang* energy.

Opposite: The entrance gate is on the White Tiger or *yin* side of the villa (left hand facing the villa). This side is elevated and more pronounced than the Green Dragon side, indicating that for the occupants, *yin* may be more dominant than *yang*.

Left: The main living room is light, bright, simple, and elegant, but richly carpeted.

Right: The country villa's main entrance. The yellow is symbolic of Earth, and the visitor must step up to the entrance, which is a traditional two-leaved door. Stepping down to the main entrance is not considered beneficial.

Left: The garden pavilion in the villa's back garden. It is reached by a wooden bridge over a water feature. In the foreground is a *yin-yang* tessellated pavement.

Right: A garden feature on the *yin* or White Tiger side of the house consists of three jars receiving water from the wall.

SANUR VILLA
GLASS WALLS AND MOATS

This villa is made up of a series of pavilions grouped around a main living pavilion and connected by wooden decking. The moat around the large living pavilion is like the embrace of a Water Dragon. These water formations are created by feng shui masters to enhance the wealth of their clients, but the dimensions and direction of flow have to be precisely calculated in order to be effective.

The Balinese stone guardian statue at the end of the driveway has the same function as a pair of Chinese lions and repels *sha ch'i* flowing in long straight lines. These ferocious guardians are often seen located at the end of dead end streets in Bali for just this reason.

Opposite: The main pavilion has a double-decked roof for better *ch'i* flow and ventilation. It is almost completely surrounded by a "moat" filled with water lilies.

Below: The main pavilion is supported by four chunky wooden pillars, and set with full length glass walls. The floor is of black and white marble tessellated pavement, strewn with rich Middle Eastern carpets.

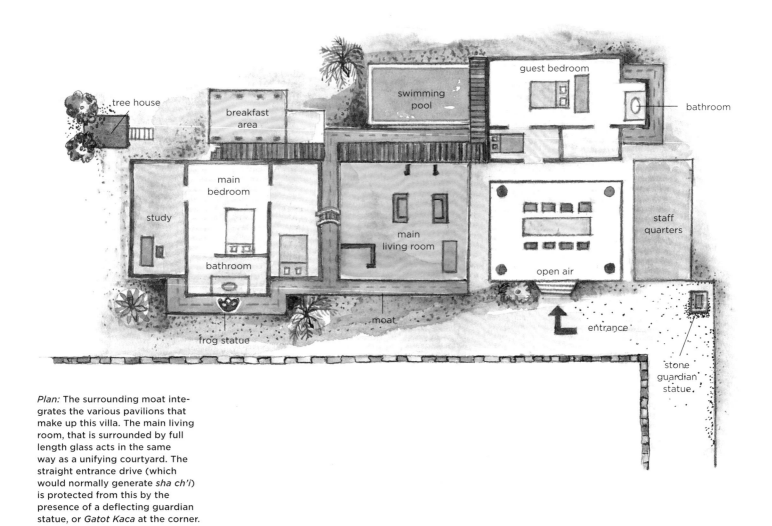

tree house

breakfast area

swimming pool

guest bedroom

bathroom

main bedroom

study

main living room

staff quarters

bathroom

open air

moat

frog statue

entrance

stone guardian statue

Plan: The surrounding moat integrates the various pavilions that make up this villa. The main living room, that is surrounded by full length glass acts in the same way as a unifying courtyard. The straight entrance drive (which would normally generate *sha ch'i*) is protected from this by the presence of a deflecting guardian statue, or *Gatot Kaca* at the corner.

Opposite: Two four-poster beds in the bedroom pavilion.

Far left: Furnishing includes this Indian divan backed by a *faux* window surround that enlivens and gives definition to the otherwise plain sheet glass windows.

Left: The sunken bath is screened by large glass windows from the continued vista of a pond presided over by a huge stone frog, a common Balinese theme.

CONTEMPORARY FENG SHUI

The best of contemporary feng shui takes the basic rules of feng shui, such as the balancing of *yin* and *yang*, or the avoidance of too many straight alignments, and combines it with clean-lined modern design. Well balanced design often achieves many of the same objectives as feng shui. Contemporary feng shui has inspired some brilliantly designed interior fountains, something not previously a feature of private Western homes. Color balance—using the model of the five Chinese Elements, Water, Wood, Fire, Earth and Metal—has provided new challenges to contemporary designers, but also brought much more meaning to the selection of color palette in specific rooms where feature walls can be used effectively to enhance different aspects of the occupants' lives.

New Age thinking however often mixes up feng shui, clutter clearing, minimalism and Zen. Most commonly, Zen minimalism and feng shui are confused. Feng shui is actually none of these. Feng shui is concerned with the objective of creating a smooth flow of *ch'i* through a building and the very real effect this has upon the health, wealth and happiness of the building's occupants. It is not concerned with the tidiness of a room, the minimalism of postwar architecture, or the spiritual clarity of Zen.

Feng shui however, discourages a completely empty *yin* space and encourages a balance between openness and more solidly furnished areas. The open areas should preferably be located in areas where good Water Stars fall, whilst the "built-up areas" should correspond with good Mountain Stars. The energy in a room has to have a clearly defined path to follow, leaving no stagnant areas.

Through deliberate organization of the orientation and functions of each room and careful calculations for placement of water features, feng shui takes over where design leaves off, enhancing the living space visually and infusing into it an invigorating energy which results in a greater feeling of confidence and well being for the occupants.

ST. ANN'S COURT
LO P'AN HOUSE

Above: The front door (positioned NE to just catch the sun on Midsummer's day) directly faces the main gates. Although in most houses the front door is also the facing direction of the house, in this case the facing is on the other side, so the main door is effectively towards the rear of the house.

Opposite: Once through the front door, a mirrored foyer duplicates the winding staircase to the next floor. The mirror is at right angles to the door, and therefore does not reflect the entering *ch'i* back out the door.

This house is one of the classics of modern architecture. It was built in 1936–37 by the Australian architect Raymond McGrath (1903–77) for Gerald Schlesinger and his partner, the landscape designer, Christopher Tunnard. The architect also worked on the classic 1930s glass designs at the BBC and RIBA in London.

The house is a real original. Its recent history includes being owned by Ray Manzanera of Roxy Music fame: in fact one of the lintels in the adjoining studio block was inscribed "Manzanera Fecit MCMLXXXIV." It has now been completely restored by the architects Munkenbeck+Marshall for its proud owners, who continue to use the studio.

The basic design of the house is that of a circle with a pie slice taken out of it. Each of its three floors adopt the same circular floor plan. The missing slice faces due south, to take full advantage of the east to west movement of the sun in the northern hemisphere. Strangely, for such a large house, it has very few rooms.

The front door, situated at the 45-degree point on the circle (remember that zero degrees marks due north) was deliberately so aligned by the architect, because he calculated that the rising sun at dawn on Midsummer's day would illuminate it.

As if self conscious of its extraordinary design, the front door faces a mosaic mirror which is etched with an illustration of the house's floor plan. Normally, a mirror directly facing the front door would not be considered good feng shui but here, the curved and fragmented nature of the mirror does not have the same effect of reflecting back out the entering *ch'i*.

There is a long-running debate in feng shui on how to divide up the house when analyzing it. Should you divide it evenly up into nine Lo Shu squares (as most traditional Chinese books on feng shui advise)? Or should you simply logically extend the radial pattern of the *lo p'an* or feng shui compass and divide the house up into eight "pie slices" (like many modern feng shui practitioners in Hong Kong do)? Traditionally, Hakka houses in Southeast China were also built in a similar circular fashion, and may have been the origin of this particular interpretation of the ancient art.

This discussion is more than just academic as the two different methods often give two different meanings to some parts of the house (even though they agree in terms of basic orientation). By designing St. Ann's Court in a circular fashion, the architect has made it very easy to use the second method of taking compass bearings from the central point of the building.

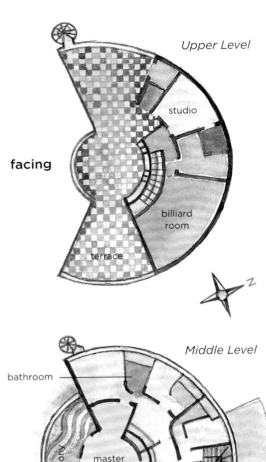

Upper Level

facing

studio

billiard
room

terrace

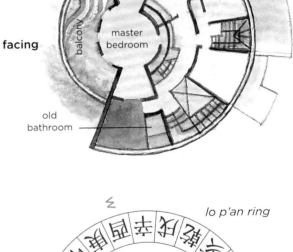

Middle Level

bathroom

balcony

facing

master
bedroom

old
bathroom

Very strangely, the architect has built the walls and divided the house as if some latter-day Hong Kong master had been present, advising him. Of course this is very unlikely, but in analyzing the feng shui of this house, it is striking that all its radial walls fall exactly on the boundaries of one of the 24 major compass divisions.

This can hardly be a coincidence, as the alignments of these walls corresponds to within half a degree in every case. Half the 24 directions are *yang* or positive, half are *yin* or negative. For example, the dining room is exactly delineated by the three *yin* directions: *mao*, *yi* and *chen* (E2, E3, SE1), the front door exactly corresponds to *ken* or NE2, and the exact north point of the top floor (the traditional direction of Water) is marked by a toilet, certainly a water feature.

St. Ann's Court's circular design could have been dreamed up simply by dividing the circle into 24 divisions. However it is a tantalizing thought that some of the travelers returning to London in those days, after a career in colonial administration, may have brought with them an example of a beautiful *lo p'an*, from which sprang the idea of building a circular house divided according to its main sectors.

lo p'an ring

Opposite: From the outside, St. Ann's Court looks completely round, with large windows that look almost industrial rather than domestic. Built of shuttered concrete, it foreshadows the English brutalist architecture of the 1960s by more than 30 years.

Plan: The circular design of St. Ann's Court is mirrored in the main ring of the feng shui compass or *lo p'an*. The south side of the house, which is opened out on both the upper and middle floors, faces the *wu* sector of the "24 Mountain" ring of the *lo p'an*. Room divisions too, follow exactly the lines of the *lo p'an* divisions.

Above: Looking up from the foyer, you are immediately struck by the clean lines, and almost ship-like handrail of the staircase and first floor. This light, white and bright entrance is designed to attract *yang* energy.

Left: The living room is backed with a large curved metal screen—the sort that would be ideal if you were trying to increase the amount of Metal energy in a room. The specially woven rug reflects the curves of the chair.

Below: Aligned exactly with the W3 sector of the west, facing the garden, is the dining room.

Opposite: The adjoining kitchen contains the few splashes of color that relieve the white of the whole building. Red is for Fire and yellow is for Earth.

Left: The master bedroom is located at the heart of the house on the middle level in the south side, and commands the wide southerly aspect. The many windows and extensive use of white makes this house a very *yang* house. In fact the bedroom, which traditionally should be a *yin* and darker room, is amongst the most *yang* of all the rooms. Even the wooden floor is rapidly being bleached to match by the sun. The result is a bedroom that is strongly *yang*, rather than the more usually advised *yin* room which feng shui suggests is best for a sound night's sleep.

Above: To the right and left of the central middle floor bedroom are two further bedrooms, and a minimalist bathroom.

Left: Directly below the bedroom, at ground level also on the south side, is a huge glassed-in living room, which is partly protected for a few weeks of the year by an ancient wisteria vine.

THE HEMPEL
PURITY OF IMAGINATION

The stark purity of the Hempel is a reflection of the taste of its uncompromising and original designer, Lady Weinberg, (*nee* Anoushka Hempel) who has broadly interpreted a number of feng shui principles in the construction of this unique London hotel. The main reception area for example, utilizes all five of the Chinese feng shui Elements, but the balance is intimidatingly *yin*, rather than the slightly *yang* balance that is needed to make such an area more inviting and comfortable.

Another basic feng shui rule to note about the design of the hotel is that the entrance to a building, which is like its mouth, should be well protected but still open enough to receive passing *ch'i* energy. This hotel has been literally hollowed out of a number of large adjoining Georgian terraces without disturbing its external domestic Victorian architectural appearance, so that a casual passerby would think that it was still a succession of ordinary residences.

Consequently, the entrance to the Hempel is hidden. It shows no more than a discreet "H" on the pillars in front of one of its Victorian-style entrances and even immediately inside the entrance room with its sea of white orchards, there is no obvious door and the room itself appears to lead nowhere. *Ch'i* needs a more obvious path to enter a building.

Opposite: The bed is suspended from the ceiling by metal rods in this suite. This is not good feng shui as sleeping over an empty space leaves one literally unsupported in daily life. Below, the low ceiling generates a distinct feeling of oppression.

Below: The five Chinese Elements are all present in the room. Water occurs in the Metal urns that are supported by the Indian Wood ox-cart. Earth is represented by the marble and Fire burns on the left.

Below and right: The black and white (and rock stars) theme is continued in the two adjoining sitting areas.

Left: Behind the head of the suspended bed, the windows open to the garden below. Traditionally, the bed should not only be well supported from below, but also well supported from behind.

Right: Some bedrooms have introduced colors like the brown of a kimono motif behind the bed to warm up the black and white.

Below left: Other bedrooms add a touch of beige (in this case in the Beluga bedroom) set off by antique Chinese chairs. The four-poster bed is traditionally frowned upon by feng shui practitioners, because it appears to be something overhanging the sleeper. Here the posts' starkness are muted by being wrapped in layers of cloth. In addition, the overhanging canopy is missing, and it is that which is usually thought to be bad feng shui, like a beam that presses down upon the sleeper and disturbs his sleep. Of course in colder climes, like England, where there used to be a lack of proper heating, the four poster provided a "room within a room" that kept its occupants warm.

Below right: Upstairs, bathrooms continue the use of appropriate feng shui, with each being equipped with metal urns, for Metal produces Water in the cycle of the five Elements.

Right: The bedrooms are each unique and differently furnished, but many repeating the black and white plus orchid signature motif.

Left: Even the corridors cleverly fold contrasting matt black square banisters round stairs lit by bright arched windows.

Below right: Even the entrance to the ensuite bathroom continues the theme of metal, in this case in the form of old motor oil containers scrubbed clean and bright. The conceptual contrast could hardly be greater, between old oilcans (perhaps one of the dirtiest things known to man in their un-cleaned state) and the clean lines and white purity of the bathroom.

Below left: Steps to the bar are made of clear plastic sandwiched between walls of pitch black, continuing the *yin-yang* contrast.

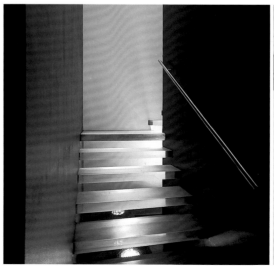

BALI BALÉ
STEPS AND STRAIGHT LINES

One of the more stunning examples of contemporary feng shui is the Bali Balé. The designers have created a series of private compounds, each with its own bed and dressing rooms, pool and outdoor balé. This whole development is tied together by a unifying flow of water down the central axis where the *yin* of the water contrasts with the *yang* of the austere white stone walls. At the entrance, the water collects in three large rectangular pools. When using water, especially on a large scale like this, it is advisable to have the water appear to flow inwards, thus drawing in the *ch'i*. The same is true of entrance fountains: they should point inwards, as water flowing out symbolizes loss of wealth.

Opposite: Water flows in a channel down the central axis of the Bali Balé grounds, flowing towards the entrance where it collects in three large rectangular pools.

Below: Each villa is equipped with a delightful open-air reading bed in a separate private balé that is shielded from rain.

Right: On the streets of the villages in Bali, most long roads or even tiny alley-ways that come to an abrupt stop at an L-bend or T-junction, are thoughtfully ended by a small temple or votive pillar. In the case of an L-bend, there may even be two separate pillars dealing will the arrival of *sha ch'i* from both directions. This well demonstrates that the Balinese understand the classical feng shui undesirability of long stretches of straight road, and that something needs to be put at the end of such a road to absorb the *sha ch'i*. Here, carved stone frogs perform the same function.

Far left: Ducks were one of the few quirky concessions to trivial decoration that this otherwise strictly minimalist place makes.

Left: The pool is *yin*, contrasting with the *yang* of the steps and massive stone walls.

Plan: Water forms the radial axis of the Bali Balé, running through a series of straight surface and hidden channels from the main pool on the left, to the reception pools located near the entrance. Individual compounds for guests flank either side of the water axis. A curved path for this water flow might have improved the overall feng shui of the compound.

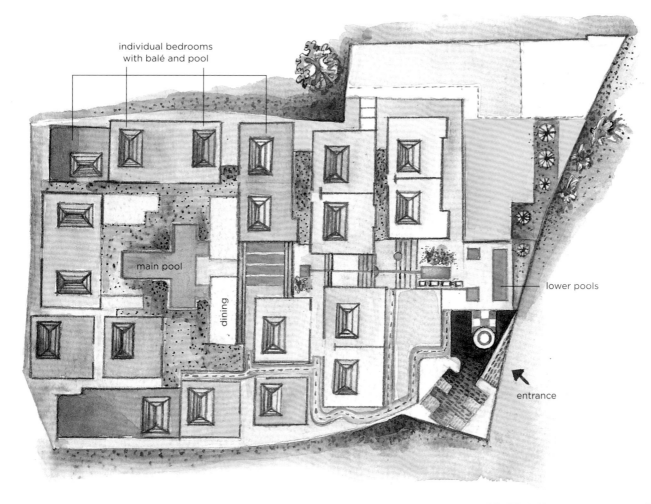

individual bedrooms with balé and pool

main pool

dining

lower pools

entrance

Left: The apparent water source is a plain dark round *yin* pond with no activity. A fountain at this point (as well as the light), would have enlivened the feng shui.

Below: The pool terminates in the plainest of square-columned gazebos.

Far below: The water descends in a straight line without any elegant curves, to the lower collecting pools. Usually feng shui dictates that water should flow sinuously, as in nature, rather than in straight lines that allow the *ch'i* to flow away too rapidly.

Above: The water-carrying wall channel is aimed like an enormous *sha*-generating arrow at the reception area.

Left: The play of light and shade, and the square lines of the pillars, softened by slatted wood in the foreground, admirably sums up the design philosophy of the Bali Balé.

Below left: Outside a villa in the grounds of the Bali Balé.

Below right: Even the patterns of sun and shadow in the main corridor of the reception area take on a highly disciplined form.

Right: In the bedroom, the theme of minimalism and perfectly squared symmetry is retained. The bedroom's perfection of line is relieved by the rustic *alang alang* grass roof that is supported by many bamboo poles tied to a high-pitched frame. The owners have resisted the temptation of putting in a white ceiling.

SANDERSON
BRIGHT YANG AND DARK YIN

Distorted scale and a clash between *yin* and *yang* are a trademark of Philippe Starck's design at the Sanderson. This is not the comfortable scented ambience of New Age feng shui, nor is it the careful balancing of *yin* or *yang* that is part of traditional feng shui. This is feng shui clearly designed to shock and stimulate, to keep the occupants awake and wondering, but function just as effectively. Here there is no escape, and the viewer is confronted. Visual puns proliferate, like the netting wrapped around a pile of rocks that turn out to be soft rubber: apparent *yang* becomes real *yin*.

The snooker room for example, has been designed and decorated as a very decadent and *yin* room, using animal horn and hoof furniture (*yin* by its association with death), mauve tones and no external daylight. This opens directly on to the white muslin brightness of the main reception: this is a man who knows how to make *yin* confront *yang*, and to disturb his viewers.

Strangely the building has a square central courtyard that in concept would not be out of place in a Classical Chinese house. This area, with its garden and fountain, is a legacy of the original 1960s design that has not been improved upon by Starck. Here water flows and plants grow in a natural setting, which in itself is a contrast with the building's interiors.

Above: A sense of unease is generated by a hard log seat and a classic 1960s hanging plastic bubble chair, too small for anyone but a child. The black Bakelite phone adds a sense of temporal confusion.

Left: A chaise lounge scaled to normal height, which should normally seat two or three people, runs 30 feet along one wall. Its back is not "supported" by the billowing muslin.

Opposite: In another corner, chairs are grouped uneasily as if huddled together to face a common enemy, with none placed so that a conversation can be held between their occupants.

Left: The center of the building is occupied by a courtyard like that of a traditional Chinese house, with a mass of greenery and running water from a stone monolith.

Right: The square sheet of water which joins the main pool at right angles, contrasts with a huge smooth boulder that sits beside the water a bit like a Brancusi egg.

Plan: The feng shui design of the Sanderson is focused around its interior garden, an equivalent of the courtyard in a traditional Chinese mansion. The pool room provides a dark *yin* contrast to the very *yang* light white areas of the long bar and reception, thus providing a balance. The sofa and curtain blocks the direct access path of *ch'i* from the main entrance.

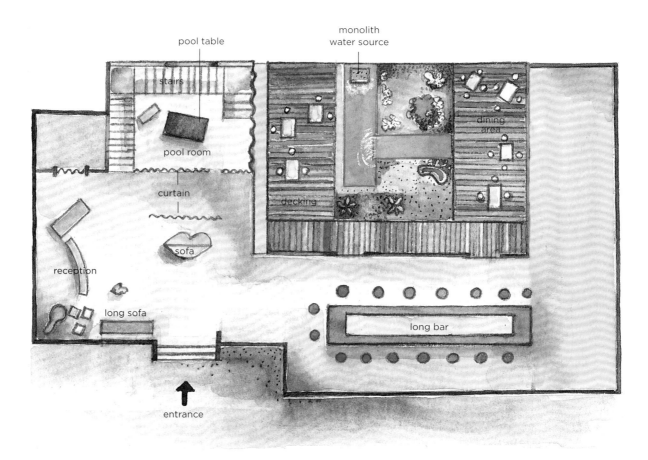

pool table

monolith
water source

stairs

pool room

dining
area

curtain

decking

sofa

reception

long sofa

long bar

entrance

Right: The snooker room is a very *yin* room. External light is filtered through a dark wall-size stained glass window. The table, covered with mauve baize, a very *yin* color, rests on a dark carpet.

Below right: The bedroom opens onto a wooden decked balcony that is screened by thickly growing bamboo. Bamboo is a symbol of growth, and can be used successfully to stimulate the Wood Element.

Left: The bathroom is composed solely of steel and glass. The hand basin is literally just a basin. The steel table is bolted to the floor at a deliberately oblique angle, with trapped space behind it.

DESIGNED FOR FAME & FORTUNE

Fame always needs a bit of luck as well as talent, and feng shui can be utilized to promote this luck. Luck after all is really just availability of opportunity. In simple Eight Mansion or *pa chai* feng shui, fame is attributed to the south sector. The Element of this direction is Fire, and its color is red. To stimulate the fame sector, you should look at decorating this area of your house or living room with the reddish range of the spectrum, with objects that relate to Fire, like red candles, bright lights or even one of those faux flames (if you have concerns about live candles). Because in the Production Cycle of the five Elements, Wood feeds Fire, so live wood in the form of indoor plants can also be helpful. A "fame" wall with cuttings and relevant photos can be useful in this sector too. Of course, you still have to put in the work and do the necessary promotion.

Fame often leads on to fortune, but if you are more interested in achieving prosperity than attaining fame, then the correct Eight Mansion sector to stimulate is the SE where the appropriate Element to activate is Wood. Support this with plenty of flourishing plants like bamboo and include a water feature, because Water produces Wood. A small indoor fountain with moving water will do nicely. It is important not to let the water turn foul or stagnate.

If you are looking to produce your wealth on a much grander scale, like the first of our examples, then you will need to engineer larger water features in the correct position. For a retail operation, much of the important feng shui is focused on the entrance in order to lure customers in. In such instances, inward facing fountains are useful, but need to be positioned carefully.

Using Flying Star feng shui calculations, the Water Star to stimulate between 2004 and 2024 is Water Star 8, but this will be found in a different position in each building or home, and its precise location needs to be calculated with reference to the facing direction of the building and the Period it was built in.

DAILY EXPRESS BUILDING
DESIGNED FOR PROSPERITY

This building used to be the headquarters of the Daily Express Newspapers, who were a very successful UK newspaper company whilst they were resident there. Subsequently, the building was taken over as the UK headquarters of a well-known merchant bank.

Built in the early 1930s in Art Deco style, the building was the brainchild of architects Herbert Ellis and William Clarke with Sir Owen Williams. From a feng shui point of view, perhaps the most important part of a building is its entrance and foyer. The foyer of this building was designed with a very strong Water theme—a true classic of feng shui design—by Robert Atkinson. The present owners however, have seen fit to use an adjacent and less impressive foyer as their main entrance, consequently losing out on the feng shui benefits of the original foyer.

The Element of Water is understood to correspond to wealth, and this foyer literally swims in it. The floor, in various shades of blue and black, has a ripple pattern so that it looks without any stretch of the imagination, as if the foyer is awash with water. This helps, from a feng shui point of view, to generate wealth for the company occupying the building and using this foyer.

The traditional quarter for Water is the north, and the building very appropriately "sits" in the north, facing south. Blue and more particularly, black, (in traditional Chinese thinking) are the colors associated with the Element Water and the north, and the décor is a combination of these two colors. Whether the architect and designer constructed this magnificent foyer with feng shui principles in mind, or whether they just managed to accidentally create an example of near-perfect Art Deco feng shui, we may never know. It seems unlikely to be a coincidence. Of all the examples of feng shui style in the present book, this is perhaps the most perfect example in the UK from the 20th century.

The building itself "sits" in the north and faces south, further confirming the rightness of its feng shui. It was built in Period 4 which runs from 1924 to 1944. If the sitting direction is taken as N1, then the foyer has a Flying Star

Left: The Water floored foyer leads to the inner (northerly) entrance that is flanked by two silver snakes. This inner entrance leads to a spiral staircase (see page 110) that winds all the way up through the floors to the outside sky. Access to the sky is a very important feng shui feature almost never seen in modern architecture, till the glass atrium became popular in the last two decades of the 20th century.

Right: The building presents a very strong presence, and it must have seemed very modern when it was first built in the 1930s. The facade is covered with black Vitrolite and clear glass with chromium strips. Water is traditionally seen as black, and as Metal "produces" the Element Water, so the façade strongly generates that Element. The five main stripes of black across the front echo the five Elements, with rows of panels in which nine (the strongest *yang* digit) features prominently.

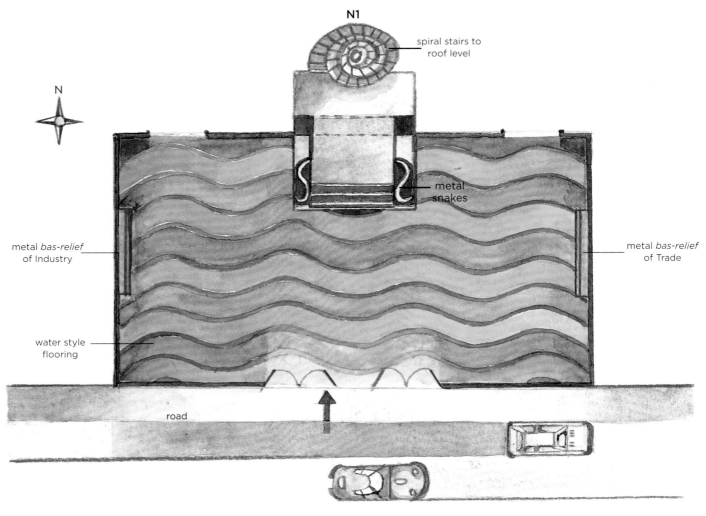

N1

spiral stairs to
roof level

metal
snakes

metal *bas-relief*
of Industry

metal *bas-relief*
of Trade

water style
flooring

road

S1

configuration of 4-8-4. In other words, both the Mountain Star 4-green and the Water Star 4-green are at the entrance. This is particularly interesting in a Period 4 building, these are the most significant stars to have at the entrance.

Furthermore the 4-green Water Star relates to income and profit through literary works, which is precisely what a newspaper aims to do in the broadest sense. The 8-white is of course also a beneficial Flying Star, making this entrance a highly desirable one from the feng shui point of view.

As Period 7 rolled around in 1984, the energy of these Stars turned neutral. It is no coincidence that in 1989, the Daily Express moved out of this classic Fleet Street building when the former energy of the building had been exhausted. The arrival of Period 8 in February 2004, with 8-white in the central Palace, will see the energy levels increasing, but a small feng shui adjustment needs to be made to prevent the star of this Period being locked in the Central Palace.

Right: One of two original plaster *bas-relief* of Trade and Industry personified, by Eric Aumonier. This one personifies Trade, with a significant nod towards the Asian colonies of the time which contributed so significantly to the wealth of Great Britain in that era.

Far right: The metal ceiling gathers into the centre in a pendant feature that looks for all the world like a stalactite-like lantern ever ready to collect symbolically condensed water.

Left: The Celestial Animal of the north is the combination of the tortoise and the snake. In the Production Cycle of the five Chinese Elements, the Element Water is produced by Metal. Here, two stylised metal snakes flank the inner entrance, generating yet more of the Water Element. The feng shui symbolism could not be more overt if it wanted to be.

Plan: Water is the key feng shui Element of this foyer. It is portrayed symbolically by the alternating black and blue wave pattern floor design. Water is also symbolically generated by Metal that has been used on all the walls and ceiling. At the sitting side, a spiral stair gives access to the sky, similar to a traditional Chinese mansion.

CHINA WHITE
CHASING THE DRAGON

This world famous nightclub under the Café Royal in London first opened its doors in December 1998. By February the following year, it had become the talk of the town and a hangout for celebrities like Madonna and Michael Jackson. Maybe it was the promotion, maybe it was the location, or just maybe it was the extensive feng shui work done on the club before it was opened by Renuka, that propelled it from new club to "it" club.

Because it is housed in an underground venue, you would expect the club's energies to be very *yin* in nature and therefore not particularly good feng shui for attracting fame. In addition, it had a small entrance down a narrow lane, adding to the constrictions and formidable feng shui difficulties to be overcome. This meant that much more had to be done than the usual feng shui consultation would require. Feng shui enhancers therefore had to be correspondingly more pronounced. *Ch'i* had to be encouraged to enter and descend through the curving staircase into the club. Enhancers were even used in the toilets to suppress *yin* energy. The general color scheme featured a lot of red and yellow, red being appropriate symbolically for the Fire Element needed for fame.

Left: The octagon room, which is meant as a chill out area, a kind of retreat or conversation area, is deliberately very *yin* in color and lighting. The eight sides suggest the *pa kua* or eight Trigrams so important in feng shui.

Right: Where one might hang just one windchime in a home, here a row of them was used (in the appropriate sector of course). Where one might place a small dragon statue beside a wall, here the main room has a full-length sandstone dragon carved along one wall. The dragon is one of the four Celestial Animals associated with the east.

Right: The Mao room, hidden behind the stone dragon, is reserved for special guests and celebrities. The Chairman probably would not have approved.

Opposite: The lower entrance area is bordered by a standing stone carved dragon.

Plan: The Mao celebrity lounge is deliberately located in the NW, the area of mentors. The dance floor is located in the SW, associated with romance. The Wu-wu chill-out room and toilets (not shown) are located in the SE sector (to the right of the plan). The draining effect of the toilets had to be carefully suppressed to prevent symbolic loss of money.

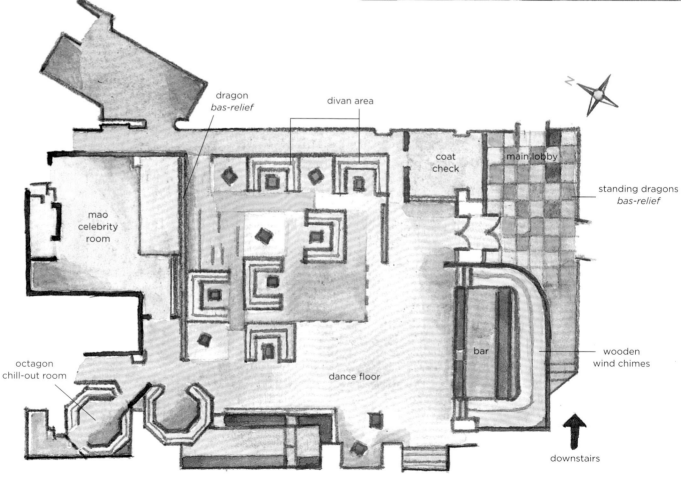

dragon *bas-relief*

divan area

coat check

main lobby

standing dragons *bas-relief*

mao celebrity room

bar

wooden wind chimes

octagon chill-out room

dance floor

downstairs

Left: The semi-private Wu-wu room is kept intimate by the use of a tented ceiling.

Below: A corner of the main room is designed in a divan style.

CHEF WAN'S PENTHOUSE
COOKING UP FAME

Simplified Eight Mansion feng shui theory ascribes each of the traditional life aspirations to one of the eight compass directions. Achieving fame, of course, takes a lot of dedication and hard work, and for most of us, the "fame" represented by this sector simply means peer recognition. As we have already seen, fame needs the Fire qualities of the south side of your living room stimulated.

Fame also depends upon your contacts, so it is advisable to stimulate your mentors area, which is associated with the NW sector of your house and the Element Metal. Use metallic colors in this area, and place actual earth here in the form of crystals or aesthetically appealing rocks, because Earth generates Metal in the Production Cycle of the Elements. Metal related decorations are also appropriate here.

A wall containing the trophies or achievements associated with your success, like framed newspaper cuttings is an effective tool too. Chef Wan has one such wall on his landing stairs. He also has on a larger scale and dominating both levels of his penthouse, a curved white wall set with a number of alcoves, and in each of which is a memento or favorite item. This wall works on the same principle.

Chef Wan's apartment reflects the many facets of his personality as well as his natural sense of style and placement. Because he is a chef, the feng shui of his kitchen is particularly important. There are a number of feng shui rules concerning the kitchen. Because the kitchen is a room where there is real fire and water, you should be careful not to cause a clash between these Elements. For example, the stove (Fire) should never directly face or even sit alongside the dishwasher, refrigerator or sink (Water). Try not to place your stove in the NW corner of the kitchen, as this is thought to "burn" the luck of the family breadwinner.

Far left: Chef Wan himself in a familiar pose.

Left: What initially might look like a cluttered living room is relieved by a great sense of color and matching themes.

Right: The end of the lounge features a wall of brightly illuminated niches containing items that are both beautiful and of personal significance. Family and friends feature in the gilt-edged photographs on the table, which would (in simple Eight Mansion feng shui) be associated with the east side of a room. The jar in the foreground is decorated with the Chinese characters for "double happiness." This room can also be overlooked from bedroom on the upper level, so that its feature wall benefits both rooms. The balcony garden leads off to the left.

Left: The kitchen is usually considered in feng shui to be one of the key rooms in the house as it is the center of nourishment.

Below: A balcony has been turned into a micro-garden with flowers, shrubs, and even windchimes. Fruit in the bowls symbolizes prosperity and plenty. The feature table is octagonal, just like the *pa kua* or eight Trigrams diagram so important to feng shui.

Far below: Although the bed in Chef Wan's bedroom has four posts, it does not have an oppressive canopy, and so does not suffer from the feng shui caution against four-poster beds.

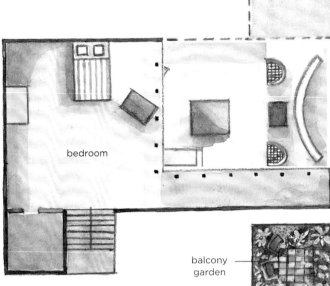

Upper Level

bedroom

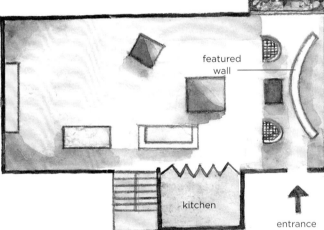

balcony garden

Lower Level

featured wall

kitchen

entrance

Plan: Both the upper and lower levels are dominated by the curved white wall (to the right). This is inset with mementos and *objets d'art* and acts as a focus point for fame aspirations. The upper level bedroom area has a balcony that gives command of the lower level living area, and the exterior balcony has been made into a garden.

LES PORTE DES INDES
RISING FORTUNES

Water is a significant part of feng shui and relates directly to wealth. Small well-placed water features like indoor fountains or aquariums are definitely beneficial. But when it comes to attracting customers and generating turnover on a large scale, then a larger water feature is called for. This central London restaurant is unique in having a large internal waterfall that connects two of its floors, giving the waterfall a considerable drop.

The water flows in a thin but wide curtain without splashing, down three panels of marble that is inlaid with alternating black and white chevrons. The Chinese Element of Water is symbolized by black, and that of Metal is symbolized by white. The Element Metal helps to generate Water. This sleek skin of water constantly passing over black and white chevrons also generates considerable *ch'i*, cooling the air, enlivening the restaurant, and increasing wealth for its owners.

The entrance area also uses still water in a broad circular Indian bronze urn to attract customers through the door. Besides floating flowers, the surface of the water also holds a candle flame, to help activate the water. There is also a large empty black earthenware jar that has been strategically located for the purpose of trapping any inauspicious energies.

Left: The top of the two-storey waterfall which uses black and white marble chevrons to energize the water flowing down over it to te pool below. The mirror behind (also a water feature) reflects the opposite wall.

Right: Immediately inside the front door is a large pottery jar, reminiscent of similar jars placed inside entrances in Bali to trap undesirable influences entering the front door. Here, performs the same function. Just beyond this is an Indian stone archway marking a formal entrance.

Plan: This restaurant is spread over several levels, with the bar area on the lowest level, so that customers and energy entering at the reception flow downwards. The feng shui focus however is on the double storey waterfall, which unites both floors and energises the *ch'i*. Water is also used in several urns near the entrance to help draw in customers.

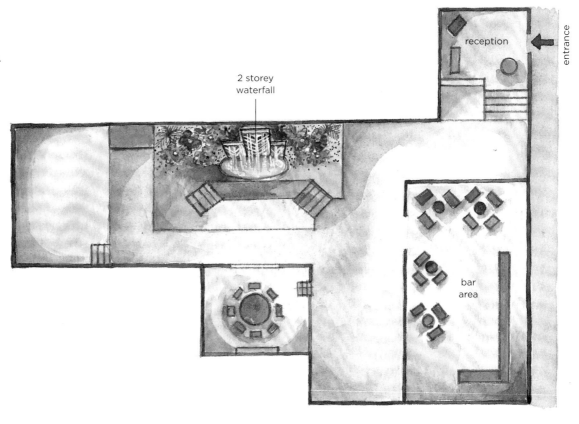

reception

entrance

2 storey waterfall

bar area

Opposite: Beyond the entrance is a large Indian bronze bowl filled with water on which are floated flower petals and a lighted candle which energizes the water.

Left: Corners hold some surprise Indian statuary.

Far left: Superb tropical flower arrangements decorate mirrors that reflect the food on the tables. It has been said that doubling the food by reflection, doubles the prosperity of a dining room.

GARDEN FENG SHUI

Feng shui is rooted in the landscape. Originally, the work of the feng shui master was to look for an ideal site or *hsueh* in the countryside where his client would either build or bury, to his best advantage. This "it" spot was where he determined that the greatest concentration of beneficial *ch'i* would be found.

The characteristics that he looked for in this piece of land were that it must face water (preferably a meandering stream, not too swift, not too stagnant), have a supporting mountain behind it, be embraced by two inward curving hills to the right and the left (like the arms of a croissant), have soil that is rich and air that is sweet with gentle breezes—not too much to ask for in the country, but sometimes impossible to find in the city. But even in cities the effects of surrounding landform on the feng shui of a building are just as important as they are in the countryside.

Cities require feng shui calculations that are based on the position of other buildings, flyovers and roads. In cities,

the tall buildings become the mountains and the roads become the rivers, although long straight roads are known to generate *sha ch'i* rather than bring benefits. In big cities nowadays, there is not the flexibility to choose the correct spot, nor is there the abundant natural energy of the surrounding countryside to replenish a building's energies. But in every city there is often to be found a little piece of the country: it is the garden.

Gardens can have a huge effect upon the feng shui of adjacent buildings, and gardens have the advantage of being more easily configurable than buildings. So if you are lucky enough to have a garden or face one, give it as much if not more feng shui thought than your home. When you are calculating directions in the garden do not use the Later Heaven sequence *pa kua* arrangement that is normally used indoors. Use instead the Former Heaven sequence that has *Ch'ien* (the Trigram with three solid lines) directly opposite *K'un* (the Trigram with three broken lines).

ST. ANN'S COURT GARDEN
INVITING THE WHITE TIGER

The landscape designer Christopher Tunnard designed this garden in the 1930s, at the same time as the house itself was being built. Although he lived in the house and enjoyed his garden for a short time, it was not long before he set off for America, never to return.

The focus of the main garden was the open downhill slope to the south of the house, forming a huge open *ming tang* in front (to the south side) of the house. Near to the circular fronted living room he planted a wisteria. Beyond that you can see, in the picture on the left, he created a stone walled pool. The pool is half-circle shaped, mimicking the circular shape of the house. Traditionally such a pool is placed in front of a house. However, it is more likely to have its curved side facing away from the house. Beyond that are carefully planted trees.

A second informal pool, with curves that also reflect the house is located to the SE. This pool had been allowed to silt up, impairing the feng shui of the house. This has now been cleaned, and is surrounded by informal plantings.

If you are designing a garden, then traditional Chinese cultural symbolism suggests types of plants that could be used. For example, the "three fortune fruits" of pomegranate, peach and finger-lemon are a popular combination.

Many houses show interesting correlations between the lives of their occupants and the feng shui of their layouts. However, few houses are actually designed from scratch using precise readings which match the *lo p'an* or feng shui compass. From a feng shui perspective, the most interesting feature of this house is the part of the garden immediately adjacent to the west of the house. This westerly garden has been very precisely located in an exact 15-degree-wide wedge of paved and walled area radiating out from the house, and corresponding exactly to the W3 direction (from 277.5 to 292.5 degrees). The *lo p'an* divides each of the eight compass directions into three sub-directions, making 24 divisions in all. Each of the eight directions is divided into Earth, Heaven and Man sub-directions.

This garden corresponds exactly with the third west sub-direction, or the *hsin* mountain on the main ring of the *lo p'an*. West is the direction of the White Tiger, a *yin* direction corresponding to autumn in the cycle of the seasons, while the third sub-division corresponds to Man. This gives it a peculiar *yin*-Man orientation. Part of the reason for this unusual orientation becomes apparent when one realizes that the original owners cum designers of the garden, are a gay couple.

Above: From the southeast, you can see the "pie-slice" taken out of the southern side. Here the shape is repeated in a pool whose own curves reflect those of the house.

Opposite: On the top floor, a large terrace reflects the circular design of the house below.

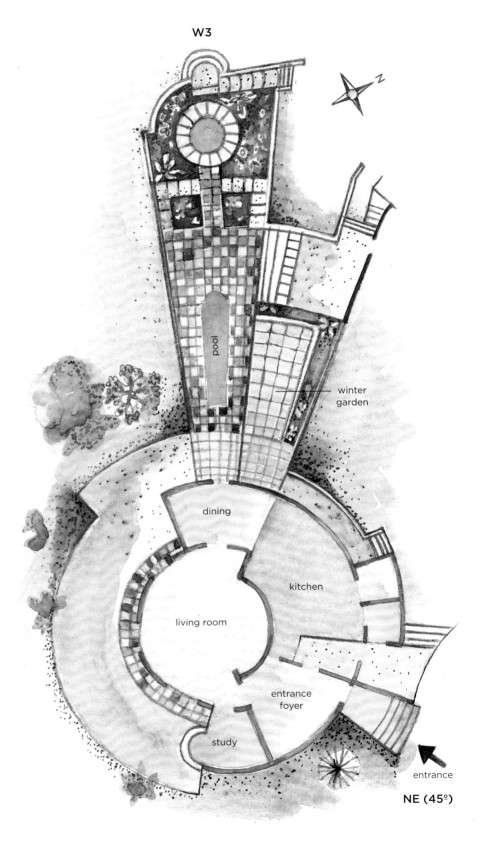

W3

winter garden

pool

dining

kitchen

living room

entrance foyer

study

entrance

NE (45º)

Above: Looking from the roof of the house, you can see how exactly 15 degrees are occupied by an enclosed garden with a long pond in its middle. The next 15 degrees round the circle are occupied by a winter garden, or glasshouse for humans rather than plants. The most important ring on any *lo p'an* or feng shui compass is divided into segments of 15 degrees and these two features, which are so important to the architecture of the house, align precisely to within half a degree with two of these feng shui sectors faning out on the White Tiger or west side of the house.

Plan: The ground floor of St. Ann's Court and its garden is designed to align exactly with the main ring of the feng shui *lo p'an* (see page 82). Other important sectors are within half a degree of its divisions. Thus, the wedge shaped garden and pool aligns with the W3 or *hsin* direction, and the winter garden aligns exactly with the NW1 or *hsu* direction.

Incorporated into this wedge is a long pool, containing a ball shaped fountain, also pointing directly to W3. Further out from the house are grassed areas surrounding a round pond, but still within this exact sub-direction. The pierced curved white wall beyond that reinforces the White Tiger association. Through the doorway pierced in this wall you can see a (modern) statue placed exactly at the W3 center point.

Adjacent to this garden is another wedge, also an exact 15 degrees (292.5 to 307.5 degrees), that corresponds with the *hsu* sector on the *lo p'an*. It contains a glassed-in "winter garden" that corresponds to the season of late autumn. To further stress the westerly alignment, the whole house is painted white, the color symbolic of that direction.

Below left: Looking out from the house, showing the exact alignment of the pool, fountain and doorway to the garden and statue beyond, aligned exactly on the W3 sector.

Below right: The perspectival precision of this feng shui water feature is clearly shown when looking back along the pool to the west side of the house.

HEMPEL GARDEN
ROUND HEAVEN AND SQUARE EARTH

This garden, made famous by its appearance in the film *Notting Hill*, belongs to the Hempel and occupies the center of the London square faced by that hotel. As such, the garden provides the hotel with an extended *ming tang* in front of its entrance. Because of the early planning of London and the way the property is owned, there is the near certainty that this garden will never be built upon. Such semi-private garden squares are common in many parts of London, and properties facing them enjoy considerable benefit to their feng shui.

This arrangement is reminiscent of the ex-headquarters building of the HSBC bank in Hong Kong, where the bank bought the open land in front of its building, and then donated it to the government with the restriction that it is to remain a public park and never be built upon.

The theme that predominates in the Hempel garden is the square and the round. In traditional Chinese cosmology, square represents Earth whilst round relates to Heaven. Parallels can be found between this garden and feng shui

cosmology, although that is not to say that these were consciously applied by the garden designer. There are three square ponds dominating the center of the garden and these reflect the threefold view of the universe which divides everything up into Heaven, Earth and Mankind. The central pond (which might represent Mankind) is larger and surrounded by gravel. On this gravel verge are placed white stone balls very much like the circles of the Ho T'u diagram in its original form, although the similarity is probably just coincidental. The Ho T'u is the origin of the earliest circular arrangement of the eight Trigrams, and shows the original balance of the Trigrams and their Elements. This pool has five circles on the north and south side of its central square, the same as the Ho T'u diagram.

The borders of the garden are marked by a hedge within which is a perimeter gravel path. This is punctuated at intervals by plants in tubs, and linen set table and chair groups. Their formality reminds one of the formal gardens of Paris like the Tuilleries.

Left: The central pool is surrounded by carved stone balls. These are carefully placed in a numerically significant pattern reminiscent of the feng shui Ho T'u square.

Plan: These three symmetrical square pools provide a serene frontage for the Hempel, and effectively provide a *ming tang* to accumulate *ch'i*. The entrance to the Hempel needs to be positioned directly opposite the garden entrance, and must be sufficiently large to take advantage of this accumulated energy. Here, it is well shielded from the activity and energies of the surrounding road by a hedge.

road

Left: Two small square pools are set either side of a central pool. This garden may be familiar to readers who may have glimpsed it in the film *Notting Hill* (where it was the scene of the wedding), although of course it is not located in that particular London suburb, but in an adjacent one.

Below left: The stone balls.

Below right: The central pool is directly in line with the entrance to the garden and faces the front door of the Hempel, making for excellent feng shui positioning.

Right: Outside in the garden, a sense of unreality of the *Mon Oncle* variety prevails. Around the edge of the garden are scattered tables that look as if they are awaiting a tea party.

KYOTO GARDEN
FENG SHUI JAPANESE-STYLE

The Kyoto Garden in London was created by ten Japanese gardeners, working to rules which were derived from Chinese feng shui. The garden is laid out in a carefully demarcated area around a double pond that is fed by a small waterfall. The three-step waterfall is flanked by two large bracketing stones (*waki ishi*). There are very specific rules governing the height of the drop—it has to be greater than 0.9 meters to be effective, or ideally, between 1.2 and 1.5 meters high. The source of the waterfall should be carefully hidden, and there are special formulas about how to set the waterfall facing the moon on specific days.

Along the sides of the pond are to be found various different types of edging, displaying the main techniques ranging from large individually chosen rocks, small vertical edging stones, hammered-in bamboo stakes, a wetlands area, and a carefully laid cobble stone "beach." As focal points, two small islands (*shima*) occupy the center of each part, one of which is made of three vertically placed stones.

The end of the pond has a stone slab bridge. Its deliberate discontinuity reflects the feng shui principle of not having a continuous straight span over water.

At two focal points on the waterside are located Japanese stone *yakumi* lanterns, one tall, one lower, which are designed to be lit at night, and reflect at just the right angle in the water's surface.

Opposite: The waterfall that feeds the whole garden and pond complex. Note the two guardian rocks on either side, whose dimensions are very carefully specified in relation to the total height of the waterfall. The waterfall provides *yang* water to the more *yin* water of the pool.

Left: The traditional Japanese stone lantern is designed to be located by the side of a pool so that its flickering night light will be reflected in the water.

Right: The stone slab bridge demonstrates the desire not to build one straight span that would generate a rush of *ch'i* at either end. Unfortunately, a safety conscious official has insisted upon filling the deliberate gap with a lighter colored stone to prevent less aware viewers from slipping inadvertently into the water. On either side, the path is made of rounded stepping stones to provide a contrast with the rectilinear austerity of the bridge.

Far right: Carefully laid cobble shore leads the eye to a stone lantern and autumnal colored trees.

Opposite: Striking maple surrounded by an informal mix of rocks and garden.

Plan: A range of typical feng shui features, from the "Buddhist trinity" stone island on the right (also seen in the photo opposite) to the discontinuous bridge (designed to prevent the generation of straight line *sha ch'i*) are seen here. Two lanterns are strategically placed to provide reflections from the pond and waterfall at night.

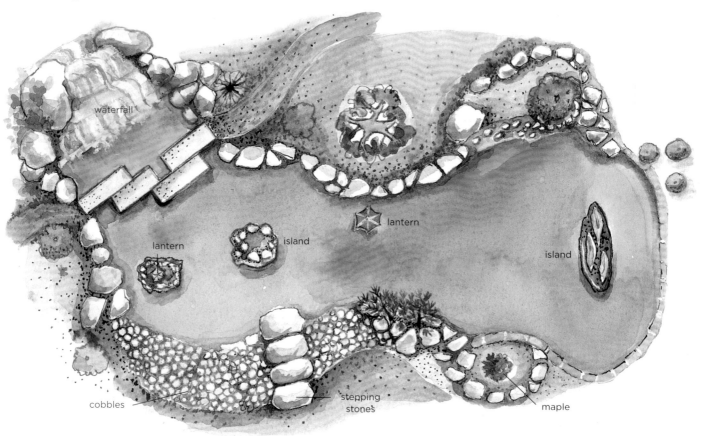

waterfall

lantern

lantern

island

island

cobbles

stepping stones

maple

ACKNOWLEDGEMENTS

Many thanks to Helen Oon, travel writer and PR person extraordinaire, who helped greatly in putting this book together, both in terms of finding suitable homes to shoot, and in coming up with simple approaches to the feng shui features of many of the places visited. My thanks also to Malaysia Airlines who allowed us to shoot their Golden Lounge at Terminal 3 Heathrow, and who were so helpful when it came to ferrying masses of photographic equipment round the world. Also to Czarska of 9–15 Neal Street, Covent Garden, London WC2H 9PW who designed this lounge and were helpful with other suggestions.

Particular thanks to Lim-Loh Lin Lee & Lawrence Loh, the architects who restored Cheong Fatt Tze Mansion to its former glory, and who were unstinting of their time. The mansion can be visited at 14 Leith Street, 10200, Penang, Malaysia (Tel: 604-262 0006, Fax: 604-262 5289, www.cheongfattzemansion.com). In the same city, which still retains so many wonderful buildings and an ongoing interest in feng shui, I wish to thank the Trustees of the Leong San Tong Khoo Kongsi Clanhouse which is open to the public at 18 Cannon Square, 10200 Penang Malaysia (Tel: 04 261 4609, Fax: 04 262 2591).

Of the private owners of premises photographed in this book, I would like to thank Shukri Shafie (of Senta Saujana), Dr Peter Worm (of Villa Hutan Datai) and Chef Wan, all of whom went out of their way to be helpful. Professor Jimmy C S Lim of CSL Associates, 8 Jalan Scott Brickfields, 50470 Kuala Lumpur, Malaysia (Tel: 603 2274 2207, Fax: 603 2274 3519, email: cslcyy@tm.net.my) was most enlightening about both ancient and modern tropical architecture, and kindly arranged for us access to the Sanur Villa as well as his own home.

Every help was extended by the owners of resorts which included Pangkor Laut, Pulau Pangkor, Malaysia; the Balé at Nusa Dua 80363, Bali, Indonesia (Tel: +62 361 775111, Fax: +62 361 775222, www.slh.com, email: jlcalle@thebale.com); and Begawan Giri (Tirta-Ening and Bayugita villas) PO Box 54 Ubud 80571, Bali, Indonesia (Tel: +62 361 978888, Fax: +62 361 978889, www.begawan.com) and its very helpful PR person, Anez Taufic.

In London, the owners of St. Ann's Court were kind enough to let us look right over their extraordinary house, plans of which were provided by their architect, Munkenbeck+Marshall Architects Ltd of 135 Curtain Road, London EC2A 3BX, UK (Tel: +44 (0)20 7739 3300, Fax: +44 (0)20 7739 3390, www.mandm.uk.com).

Lastly, I would like to thank the owners and management of the former Daily Express Building, Fleet Street, London; China White, 6 Air Street London W1R 7HH (Tel: 020 7343 0040, Fax: 020 7343 0041, www.chinawhite.co.uk); Les Porte des Indes, 32 Bryanston Street London W1H 7EG (Tel: +44 (0)20 7224 0055, Fax: +44 (0)20 7224 1144, email: london@laportedesindes.com); and The Hempel, 31-35 Craven Hill Gardens London W2 3EA (Tel: +44 (0)20 7298 9000, Fax: +44 (0)20 7402 4151, www.the-hempel.co.uk).